# Be
# JOYful...
## Who Me?

*Jesus said,*
"I love you! Remain in my love." *"I have told you this
so that my joy may be in you and that your joy
may be complete." (John 15:9, 11)*
Therefore, *fix [your] eyes on Jesus, the author
and perfecter of [your] faith, who for the joy
set before him endured the cross… so that you will not
grow weary and lose heart. (Hebrews 12:2a, 3b)*
Jesus guarantees that *in His presence
there is fullness of joy. (Psalm 16:11)*

*Annetta E. Dellinger*
Joyologist

Joy Burst Publishing
United States of America

I

Scripture quotations

Stories and quips included in this book have been collected over a long period of time and we have diligently tried to identify the material's origin. Where no source is named, the writer is unknown, and the author disclaims any ownership or control of rights to this unattributed material.

The author thanks the Lutheran Women's Missionary League for permission to use excerpts from eight articles she wrote during her term as Christian Living Editor of *Lutheran Woman's Quarterly*.

## Be Joyful...Who Me?

© 2004 by Annetta E. Dellinger
ISBN 0-9743653-0-0
200311570 Copyright, Library of Congress

Printed in the United States of America

Published by Joy Burst Publishing
        Plain City, OH 43064

Illustrator: Leo Richardson
Editor: Marlys Taege Moberg
Consultants: Karen Boerger, Nancy Bowman, Denise McCabe

### Popular Joyologist
### Annetta E. Dellinger
### Speaker-Author

*Available for your event*

Retreats    Convention Keynotes

Seminars    Conferences

*The Joy Lady*, Annetta E. Dellinger, known as a Bubbleologist, whose PHD stands for **P**erky **H**appy **D**isciple, is a trail blazer for joy! She is one of the most sought after names in women's ministry today. She is a motivator and an encourager, and her lively sense of humor and engaging transparent style create immediate rapport. She ignites listeners with a burning desire to develop a greater intimacy with God and find lasting joy in that personal relationship. Her messages are Biblically sound, currently relevant and power-packed as she offers audiences hope and real life applications.

Annetta is the founder and president of Joyful Ministries and a member of the National Speakers Association. She has authored 30 books, been a frequent guest on radio talk shows and published numerous articles. She gives God all the glory as He works through her to be His contagious Joy Agent!

Annetta Dellinger, Joyful Ministries
1810 Lombard Rd.
Plain City, Ohio 43064
Web: www.annettadellinger.com
e-mail: Annettadell@aol.com

MEMBER

NATIONAL
SPEAKERS
ASSOCIATION

# More Joyologists Available for Your Event

**Jan Struck**, Struck with Laughter
Christian Humorist/Speaker for Retreats, Workshops, Recognition Events

Jan has been entertaining audiences for 30 years with her humorous joy-centered approach to the day-to-day Christian journey of faith and trust. Two of the most popular characters she portrays are Gracie Ann (age 5) and Pearl (ageless) who provide a wonderfully comic view of "Serving the Lord."

> Jan Struck
> N9665 Darboy Drive, Appleton, WI 54915
> email: struckwlaughter@aol.com

**David Paul Britton**, Ministry of Musical Mission & Education (MMME)
Christian Worship Leader, Songwriter/Performer, Music Workshops

National recording artist and worship leader, David Paul specializes in services, family concerts, conventions, and educational assemblies. As a Music Missionary-At-Large, he conducts music and worship workshops throughout the United States, assisting congregations as they broaden worship styles from traditional to contemporary. He has also written and recorded numerous theme songs for Christian conventions and gatherings. His latest is "Count It All Joy." Visit his website for calendar information and music samples.

> David Paul Britton
> 1735 Hiawatha, Saginaw, Mi 48604
> email: dbritton@mmme.org
> http://www.mmme.org

**The Joyful Noiseletter**, the award-winning newsletter of the Fellowship of Merry Christians. Subscribers (churches and individuals) may reprint the monthly newsletter cartoons and jokes. 1-800-877-2757 www.joyfulnoiseletter.com

## Joy Note to the Reader

May you be blessed by the personal testimonies
that are shared with you in this book.
The writers pray that you will find hope,
encouragement and a new perspective
through their words.

## Joy Bursts to...

all God's children who humbly wrote about personal
crises in their journeys through life. Truly, it was the work
of the Holy Spirit who enabled you to share your powerful
message. I praise God for you. May God be glorified!

## Joy Sparks of Love and Appreciation...

To: John Dellinger, my husband, who faithfully and
patiently helped with this book to make it become a
reality. You are the perfect example of God's love in
action!

To: Grandchildren D.J. and Rob Dellinger, Megan and
Kirstin Marshall, and their parents: Doug and Libby
Dellinger, Laura and Mark Marshall.

To: Sharon Richardson for the book layout and her
patience.

To: Karen Boerger, Patty Boerger, Arleen Bohlmann, Nancy
Bowman, Marilyn Britton, Dolores Bruncke, Rev. Jack
Heino, Janet Hurta, Lois Hudack, Ruth Ann Johnson, Lisa
Kunze, Rev. Gerald Matzke, Marlys Taege Moberg, Mildred
Nicol, Edie Norris, Liz Renner, Jan Struck, Donna Streufert,
Maria Sutorik and many other joyful encouragers.

## About the Artist, Leo Richardson

As a part-time cartoon illustrator, Leo enjoys working with his wife, Sharon, who is a freelance graphic artist. They hope to magnify the Lord whether contributing their talents to their local church or by illustrating a book. Besides spending time with their two children, Sara and Jeremy, much of their spare time is devoted to producing a line of Christian Encouragement and Christmas cards.

Leo tries to draw his characters depicting anyone who has had to wear their earthly father's robe in their Sunday School Christmas play, but still feels part of their Heavenly Father's production.

*Encourage one another with thoughts that are excellent and praiseworthy as we see the Day approaching.*

Barnabas Cards™
Richardson Graphic/Art Studio
4889 York Road
Leicester, New York 14481
grichardson2@earthlink.net

# Table of Contents

X

XII

**Joy Booster:** Thoughts to guide us to God's unfailing love and faithfulness and reminders of how to stop the joy thieves. (Romans 8:38-39)

**Joy Burst:** The human spirit's way to express outrageous praise to God for His grace. Individuals, or Joy Bursts, each express joy in their own unique way from quiet reflection to contagious enthusiasm. (Philippians 4:4)

**Joy Buster:** Things that draw our focus away from Christ and rob us of contentment in our daily living. (Peter 5:8)

**Joy Connection:** A time for prayer, praise and thanksgiving. (Philippians 4:6-7)

**Joy-filled:** In Jesus' presence we are filled with His lasting joy. (John 15:11, Matthew 28:20b)

**Joyful:** Our response to God's grace. (Psalm 16:11)

**Joy Injection:** Scripture texts. (Psalm 119:105)

**Joy - External Joy:** Temporary. Based on changing circumstances. (Job 20:5)
    **Internal Joy:** The only permanent Source, Jesus Christ, is there in spite of circumstances. (Malachi 3:6)

**Joy-Spiration:** Connects real life applications with God's Word. Find hope, lasting joy and discover contentment because we place our trust in the Lord. (Nehemiah 8:10b)

# Abounding Joy Every Day? Yes!

## ▰ Joy Buster

**Be Joyful!**
**Who me? I live in a doom-and-gloom world.**
**How can I find joy when nothing ever stays**
**the same?**

## ▰ Joy Booster

Too often people make the mistake of living on the
happy side of life rather than on the joyous side of
life. They fix their eyes on people, events and things
that go their way. But since change is constant, people
become unhappy and look for another source to
provide that happy feeling. Unfortunately, the cycle
goes on because the world offers us only a temporary
kind of happiness.

1

Rejoice! Celebrate! There is hope. You can have real joy no matter what is happening in your life! This permanent Source of joy will not depend on things going your way. In fact, no matter how much your circumstances change, real joy will always be ready and waiting just for you. Lasting joy can only be indexed to the character of God and His presence and promises. That Source will never change; therefore, you can always have real joy.

Abounding in joy may not be easy. You will still ask, "Why?" or say, "I give up." But, be assured that since Jesus came to earth, He knows how devastating and discouraging life can be.

It takes discipline to walk by faith and to resist the spirit of despair, but opening your eyes to God's goodness stops the joy-thieves right in their tracks. Satan prowls constantly. He instigates negative thoughts and draws your mind away from Jesus.

If you are tired of being emotionally squashed by circumstances, find joy in God's Word. Marinate in His powerful promises. Be revitalized by what He has to say about the peace and joy He has for you! Be encouraged that God can even use your burdens as avenues for blessings.

Jesus' joy came from a close relationship with His Father. He wants to be close to you too. Your relationship with Him, nourished through the Word, will empower you to rise above the pressures of life that could otherwise squelch your joy. Celebrate! You can abound in joy daily because in His presence there is fullness of joy! *Grab Joy and Go - energized!*

## Joy Injection

*I have told you this so that my joy may be in you
and that your joy may be complete.*
*John 15:11*

*You have made known to me the path of life;
you will fill me with joy in your presence,
with eternal pleasures at your right hand.*
*Psalm 16:11*

## Joy Connection

Dearest Jesus,
I praise You for the real joy I find in...
Forgive me for...
Help me to make a difference today by...

**You can be happy and joyful
at the same time.
The difference is in the Source.**

# JOY Burst

## Be Joyful?
### Yes I can, even when...

If you think you've had cabin fever, listen to my story. I was confined inside for a l-o-n-g time! As if that weren't enough, it rained constantly! Before this happened, I had watched the neighbors laugh at my husband for years, and that hurt me. Because of all the rains, my home was destroyed, places I loved to visit were erased, my friends drowned, and everything was gone except for my husband Noah, our three sons and their wives. Now I understand how Noah's ark was God's refuge for us. God kept His promise that He had a plan for our lives, and He has one for your life too! Trust that He has been with you in the past, will be in the future and is with you right at this moment. That thought gives me confidence and security. I can't help but be a joy burst for the Lord because of all He does for me. Count your blessings and be a joy burst too!

* Genesis 6,7,8

Trust in the Lord, always!
*Joy Burst Mrs. Noah, Heaven*

*The Lord is faithful*
*to all his promises*
*and loving*
*toward all he has made.*
*Psalm 145:13b*

4

# Amazing Grace

## ▰▰▰ Joy Buster

**Be Joyful!**
**Who me? I've worked hard to earn God's**
**blessing – I deserve it!**

## ▰▰▰ Joy Booster

Once upon a time a college professor collected the
final exams from his students. Much to the horror of
the scholars, the teacher immediately tore them up.
"Why?" they demanded. He answered, "I wanted to
give you an example of grace. Deserve it or not, you
will each receive an A." Undeserved, that's what
makes God's grace so incomprehensible! No matter
how hard we try, there is
no one who escapes
from sinning. Yet
God bathes you daily
with His undeserved gift
of grace. His love is
unconditional and everlasting!
Never will He say, "I will
love you today *only if*
*you…*" God knows
you intimately. He hears
your requests for forgiveness.

5

He wants you to draw close to Him and fulfill the purpose He has for your life. What an awesome… mighty… faithful God you have! **Caution: Prepare for joy-sparks!** *Grab Joy and Go!*

## Joy Injection

*"My grace is sufficient for you, for my power*
*is made perfect in weakness." Therefore I will boast*
*all the more gladly about my weakness,*
*so that Christ's power may rest on me.*
*That is why, for Christ's sake, I delight in weakness,*
*in insults, in hardships, in persecutions, in difficulties.*
*For when I am weak, then I am strong.*
*2 Corinthians 12:9-10*

## Joy Connection

Almighty Father,
I praise You for the real joy I find in…
Forgive me for…
Help me to make a difference today by…

**Joy gives us the determination
to go forward even when
the way before us appears blocked.**

# And the Winner is Coffee!

## Joy Buster
**Be Joyful!**
**Who me? How can anything else happen to me?**

## Joy Booster

It had been a terrible, horrible, very bad day for a woman who thought nothing else could go wrong. Her friend suggested that she look at her circumstances in a different way. "If you would set three pans of water on the stove, one with a carrot, the second with an egg and the third, ground coffee beans; and boil each for 20 minutes, what would happen?" asked the friend. She continued, "The once strong carrot would weaken. The fragile egg would harden. The coffee beans and wonderful aroma, made the best of the situation, plus coffee! Each object faced the same adversity, boiling water, but each reacted differently. Which are you like when change happens?"*

When life is at its worst, with God's help you can change the situation by

7

changing your out-look to an up-look! Life's joy-blockers are not unbeatable. The God who lives in you is immeasurably greater than the most tenacious joy-thief you will ever encounter. Wow! What a faith-lift! *__Grab Joy and Go! Enjoy change.__*

*Adapted Author Unknown

## Joy Injection

*In this you greatly rejoice, though now for a*
*little while you may have had to suffer grief*
*in all kinds of trials. These have come*
*so that your faith—of greater worth than gold*
*which perishes even though refined by fire—*
*may be proved genuine and may result in praise,*
*glory and honor when Jesus Christ is revealed.*
*1 Peter 1:6-7*

## Joy Connection

Precious Savior,
I praise You for the real joy I find in...
Forgive me for...
Help me to make a difference today by...

# No woman ever injured her eyesight by looking on the bright side of things.

# JOY Burst

## Be Joyful?
### Yes I can, even when...

Be joyful when I can't remember where I parked my car when I walk out of a mall; when my husband smiles at me across the dinner table and tears pour down my cheeks; when I can't recall the name of a friend I've known for eight years? Fear grips me as I sit with a completely blank mind. Why is this happening to me? Something just isn't right.

I am hot most of the time, awake at 3:00 in the morning, and I feel lightheaded. I need glasses. My body has taken on a life of its own. I can't stay focused and I need lists, lots of lists. I feel as though I'm losing a grip on life.

Be joyful - who me? YES! It's what they call menopause and it is okay! I sought the advice of my physician and he verified that everything was okay. He assured me it was normal to say and do the unexpected, including "Is it hot in here or is it me?"

From that point on, I decided to ride the wave of change with two things in mind:

- First and foremost, the promise of God's grace. He has redeemed me through His Son, Jesus Christ, and that filled me with the hope of spending an eternity with Him. His grace is sufficient for me!

- Second, humor! Humor has carried me through the raising of seven children and will carry me again through menopause. When I can't find my car, I thank God for the panic button on my remote and follow the little tooting horn to my car. Tears for no reason don't alarm me anymore. I let it go and move on. When I don't remember a name, I'm grateful that some women wear sweatshirts with their names embroidered on them. I'm not afraid to tell people that I have drawn a blank and that my mind goes on an occasional vacation!

The physical changes are normal, so I just accept them. When I'm up at 3 a.m. reading a funny book, I wear a pair of funky reading glasses. I have a ball shopping for them. I try to be responsible with exercise and eating. In the mirror I see God's creation, beautiful and changing. I have a 13-year-old daughter in puberty and a 26-year-old daughter expecting twins. God has fearfully and wonderfully made us. As women we are constantly experiencing change.

To God be all glory that He is never changing! This promise assures me of His love and my salvation through Jesus Christ. Yes, I can be joyful, even in menopause because I know that the Holy Spirit empowers us each day through Word and Sacrament!

Through all life's seasons, God is there!
*Joy Burst Monica Andreasen, Iowa*

*You have made known to me the path of life;*
*you will fill me with joy in your presence,*
*with eternal pleasures at your right hand.*
*Psalm 16:11*

# As Life Turns

### ▬▬▬ Joy Buster
**Be Joyful!**
**Who me? I have so many things to focus on today, where do I begin?**

### ▬▬▬ Joy Booster

Centering clay on a revolving wheel is the first, most important, and most difficult step in using a pottery wheel. To produce a good finished vessel, this step must be practiced until perfected. Centering is an age-old problem for people too! It began in the Garden of Eden when Adam and Eve sinned. As a result you are always being pulled off center and challenged in your daily walk. Doubt it? Did one unkind word roll off your tongue yesterday? Has one jealous or selfish

 thought entered your mind today? Have you been pouting or praising God for your problems? Stay centered on Christ *first*, and then everything else will fall into place!

11

Best of all, your joy-o-meter will skyrocket! *Grab Joy and Go have a great day!*

## Joy Injection

*I said to the Lord, You are my Lord;*
*apart from you I have no good thing.*
*Psalm 16:2*

## Joy Connection

El Shaddai,
I praise You for the real joy I find in...
Forgive me for...
Help me to make a difference today by...

# When you focus on Christ you will be joy-filled - then you'll be joyful.

Annetta E. Dellinger

# Attitude Adjustment

## ▬▬▬ Joy Buster

**Be Joyful!**
**Who me? I'm disgusted – nothing's going**
**right today!**

## ▬▬▬ Joy Booster

It's not the circumstances facing you that bring you down but how you deal with them! There once was a useless mule that fell in an old well. The farmer decided that since he used neither one anymore he would fill the well with dirt. The mule kept feeling something hit him on his back. Whenever he did, he would shake it off and step up, shake it off and step up! Eventually he stepped out of the well! *

Too often we let others' values and actions dictate our attitude and behavior. While in prison Joseph could have had a negative attitude. Instead, he did his best with each small task.

Follow Joseph's example!  God can reverse even over-whelming odds! Copy Christ's attitude. Forgive those who frustrate you. Splash grace over everyone today! You'll benefit, too, and then you can…

***Grab Joy and Go!***

\*Story source unknown

## Joy Injection

> *With joy you will draw water*
> *from the wells of salvation.*
> *Isaiah 12:3*

## Joy Connection

Dearest Jesus,
I praise You for the real joy I find in…
Forgive me for…
Help me to make a difference today by…

**Joy is a choice, a matter of attitude**
**that stems from one's confidence in God…**
**that He is at work…in full control…**
**midst whatever has, is, or will happen.**

Charles Swindoll

# JOY Burst

## Be Joyful?
### Yes I can, even when...

"Accidents" are just that—unplanned events in life often with traumatic circumstances that test one's thoughts and beliefs.

One evening after weeding my perennial garden, I shut the storage shed garage door and grabbed it at the wrong place. My finger was flattened and the tip was gone!

A few horrifying and painful minutes later, I was at Urgent Care. The doctor's oral diagnosis of a "finger-tip amputation" did not ease my fears. But there was a turn of good fortune, as I listened to the doctor's phone consultation with a hand specialist.

The next morning, the hand surgeon gave me the option either to graft skin from my thigh (spot reduction, perhaps?) or attempt to reattach the severed tip. Asking his advice, the surgeon said he was a man of faith, so he stitched the fingertip back on.

When the doctor applied the Twinkie-size gauze, he said, "Absolutely no peeking for ten whole days!" Of course, this gave me time to worry if blood-poisoning would occur and if the tip would reattach itself. Along with prayers, my faith, and help from family, friends, and my husband, I learned to appreciate the "little things I took for granted"...washing my hair, dressing, cooking....

On the ninth day, I caught the gardening itch and decided to do some gentle raking. The next morning I awoke to an unveiling - as though truly a sign from God, the gauze had unwound itself. The surgeon later attested to the finger's successful healing.

While I couldn't help but wonder why this had happened (was it because I'd opted to miss choir that beautiful spring night?), it was faith and hope that supported me those ten days.

What a miracle! While the surgeon's hands did the stitching, God, with His grace and power, performed the miraculous healing. I celebrated by thanking God, receiving flowers from my husband, and then by bringing in Vienna Finger cookies to work!

God does answer prayer!
*Joy Burst Maria Bronner Sutorik,*
*Michigan*

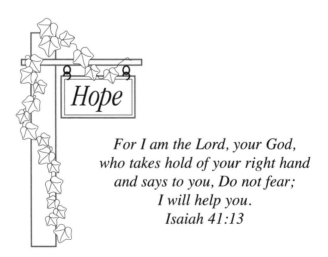

*Hope*

*For I am the Lord, your God,*
*who takes hold of your right hand*
*and says to you, Do not fear;*
*I will help you.*
*Isaiah 41:13*

# Avoid A Weight Problem!

## Joy Buster

**Be Joyful!**
**Who me? How can I when my scale is always wrong?**

## Joy Booster

Psychology Today, February 1997 issue ran an article with the results of its weight survey that asked, "How many years of your life would you trade to be at your ideal weight?" Fifteen percent of the women and eleven percent of the men said they would sacrifice more than five years of their life. Would you?

Whether you want to lose, gain or stay the same, Satan is thrilled when you focus on your physical rather than your spiritual weight. To gain weight, handle your problems all alone! To feel lighter, lay all your burdens at the foot of the cross and leave them there!

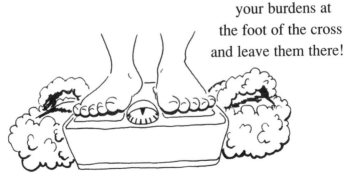

You may not always be happy with your body weight, but that never needs to rob you of God's joy! *Grab Joy and Go!*

## Joy Injection

*Turn all your anxiety over to God*
*because he cares for you.*
*1 Peter 5:7 God's Word (GW)*

## Joy Connection

Dearest Jesus,
I praise You for the real joy I find in...
Forgive me for...
Help me to make a difference today by...

The name of Jesus
is a name of joy.
When the memory
of our sins
weighs us down,
this name
brings back our joy.

# Bathe Then Shower

## ▬▬ Joy Buster

**Be Joyful!**
**Who me, when I miss my shower?**
**Did they really bathe once a week in the**
**"good old days"?**

## ▬▬ Joy Booster

Linger in the shower while the warm water trickles
over you from head to toe. Refreshing! But before you
shower, bathe in His Living Waters. Soak. Meditate.
Let God's promises and the reassurance of eternal life
trickle through your mind. Linger in the joy of knowing Him personally. Scrub your mind and heart with
the question, "How will God's Word change my day?"
The more you *know* about God's cleansing power, the
more resources you will have to *guide* you in your
daily decisions. Dry off with joy-wipes!
Live today in the joy-filled

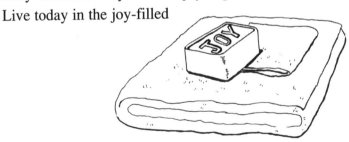

confidence of Christ's love and presence. Erupt into joy bursts! ***Grab Joy and Go.***

## Joy Injection

> *Fix these words of mine in your*
> *hearts and minds.*
> *Deuteronomy 11:18a*

## Joy Connection

Cleansing Savior,
Wash me with Your Living Waters,
I praise You for the real joy I find in...
Forgive me for...
Help me to make a difference today by...

 **Fill up your mind every morning with God's Word, then there's no room left for worry.**

# Beautiful! Make-Up or Make Over

## Joy Buster

**Be Joyful!**
**Who me? I don't like the way I look. My**
**hairstyle and make-up is outdated. I need a**
**make-over!**

## Joy Booster

Physical appearance is important, and beauty is a
lovely accessory to be enjoyed in life. After all, you
are the child of the King! Taking care of your body
indicates to God, yourself and others the value you put
on His Creation. Just as we gift-wrap presents for
others, so we should gift-wrap ourselves. The danger
comes when these things become all-consuming and
dominate the way you see yourself and others. No
amount of make-up will make a face beautiful that is
frowning in frustration,
glaring in anger or
spouting ugly
words. No amount
of make-up can
improve a face
that is shining

21

with love for the Lord! *His kind of beauty comes from the heart and lasts forever.* So try a new hairstyle, test some new cosmetic colors, but remember: make-up or no make-up, true beauty is seen when the joy of the Lord shines from within you! ***Grab Joy and Go!***

## Joy Injection

*Charm is deceptive and beauty is fleeting but a woman who fears the Lord is to be praised.*
*Proverbs 31:30*

## Joy Connection

Dear Jesus, my Foundation,
I praise You for the real joy I find in...
Forgive me for...
Help me to make a difference today by...

**There is no beautifier of complexion, or form, or behavior, like the wish to scatter joy - not pain - around us.**

Ralph Waldo Emerson

# Be Contagious!

## Joy Buster

**Be Joyful!**
**Who me? Why should I smile? After all,**
**people will wonder what I'm up to!**

## Joy Booster

If another's only view of Christ would be what they
saw in you, would they say, "I want what you have!"
Or, "I don't want any part of what makes you look so
grumpy!" It has been said that *most folks are just
about as happy as they set out to be*. Why is it that a
lot of Christians do not look like they enjoy being
God's child? Do they dwell on the sweet by-and-by
instead of the here and now? Being happy does not
mean you must have a perpetual smile. But when the
King resides in your heart, His love will uniquely

23

show in your words and body language. Don't be surprised at the smile on your face, the bounce in your walk, your encouraging words, the energy in your talk and the way you glisten with gladness. God is at work! Be a-dazzle! What's ahead for you is far beyond your wildest dreams—eternal life! *Grab Joy and Go!*

## Joy Injection

> *But the fruit of the Spirit is love, joy,*
> *peace, patience, kindness, goodness,*
> *faithfulness, gentleness, and self-control.*
> *Galatians 5:22-23*

## Joy Connection

Jesus, Man of joy, who created the smile,
I praise You for the real joy I find in...
Forgive me for...
Help me to make a difference today by...

# If you have the joy of Jesus in your soul, please notify your face.

# Be Extravagant!

## ▰▰▰ Joy Buster

**Be Joyful!**

**Who me? How can anything made from the dust of the ground be valuable?**

## ▰▰▰ Joy Booster

You may have heard the saying, "It is what's on the inside that counts!" In some countries people hide their valuable possessions in clay pots. Just like clay vessels, our bodies were created from the ground and we contain the greatest of all treasures, Jesus Christ! He has chosen us frail and fallible human beings to share the Good News, each in a way no one else does. He knew what He was doing when He combined your personality and talents. He had a *specific purpose* in mind just for you, His precious clay vessel! The Holy Spirit works through your uniqueness to put God's love in action in a way that no one else ever can. Be extravagant with this treasure!

*You contain* a never-ending supply of God's love, and He has equipped you to share it. Without Him we are nothing. But, through His Spirit we can do all things. Get out of the Secret Service business about your Savior. Share God's joy everywhere. Be contagious! Yes *you*! **Grab Joy and Go be His joy burst!**

## Joy Injection

*But we have this treasure in jars of clay*
*to show that this all-surpassing power*
*is from God and not from us.*
*2 Corinthians 4:7*

## Joy Connection

Almighty Creator,
I praise You for the real joy I find in...
Forgive me for...
Help me to make a difference today by...

# The more a person loves, the closer he approaches the image of God.

Martin Luther

## Be Joyful?
### Yes I can, even when...

I was the topic of gossip, because of my immoral lifestyle, so I avoided being around the women especially when they drew water at the well. However, one day during my routine trip at noon, a Jewish man stopped to talk to me. He asked if I would give Him a drink. I was confused. After all, I'm a Samaritan with a despicable reputation and this was a public place. Who was this man who disregarded social barriers, knew that I had five husbands and was now living with another man? He offered me a drink of Living Water that would forever quench my thirst for God.

The Messiah forgave my sins. From that moment on my life changed. I was ecstatic! I couldn't even finish filling my water pots. I raced to tell everyone (including those gossips) about the joy and freedom we have in the forgiveness of our sins.

*Don't ever think that you are unforgivable.* Jesus doesn't! I know, I'm the *Woman at the Well.* I encourage you to not just know *about* Jesus but to immerse

*Hope*

yourself in a *personal* relationship with *your* Savior!
He guarantees that your life will never be the same
and you'll be a Joy Burst too!

Jesus' love is endless!
*Joy Burst Samaritan Woman, Heaven*

*I give them eternal life, and they shall never perish;
no one can snatch them out of my hand.
John 10:28*

# Be Still

■■■■ **Joy Buster**

**Be Joyful!**
**Who me? I'm so busy, I can't remember**
**how to be still!**

■■■■ **Joy Booster**

Because a potter lives in the hope that from a shape-less lump of clay will emerge a vessel of worth, he is willing to endure the slow, tedious process of preparing the clay. Clay needs a time to rest so a more even texture and increased plasticity can take place. Rest helps you prepare physically, emotionally, mentally and spiritually for the next day. Sometimes you are forced to rest because of your child's cold or a work shut-down. To be still and be at rest is not taking away from your life journey, rather it is an important part of it. Abraham was 75 when God announced he would be a father of many nations, yet he *rested* 25 more years before Isaac was born.

*Be still and know that God is in charge.*

The Apostle Paul was ready to take a joy-leap into his ministry after his conversion. God had other plans.* *Be still and know that God is in charge.* Mentally visit Christ's open tomb and in silent awe, let the joy of Easter give you resurrection power! ***Grab Joy and Go!***

*Acts 9; Galatians 1

### ▰▰ Joy Injection

> *Be still, and know that I am God.*
> *Psalm 46:10a*

### ▰▰ Joy Connection

Dear Refuge for my rest,
I praise You for the real joy I find in...
Forgive me for...
Help me to make a difference today by...

**You may think you
are waiting for God,
but He could be
waiting for you!**

# Because I Say So

■■■■ Joy Buster

**Be Joyful!**
**Who me? I'm a parent, and it's called**
**survival of the fittest!**

■■■■ Joy Booster

God knows about your desire to be a good and godly
parent. He knows how exhausting parenting is and
how quickly words can be spoken... "I'm busy. Don't
bother me now," or "I'm the Mother, that's why!"
Keep the only parenting manual that is always current
on the table. God's Word to parents will always be
a place to fill up with guidance and joy! Beware,
though, of how quickly Satan can cause you to give
in and compromise your values when you hear,
"Everybody else is doing it. Please just this once?"
With God in your family, you can survive raising kids!
*Grab Joy and Go thank God*
*for your family!*

31

## Joy Injection

*Now you've got my feet on the life path,*
*all radiant from the shining of your face.*
*Ever since you took my hand,*
*I'm on the right way.*
*Psalm 16:11 The Message (MSG)*

## Joy Connection

I come to You, my Father,
I praise You for the real joy I find in...
Forgive me for...
Help me to make a difference today by...

**If the future generations
were dependent on you
for spiritual knowledge,
how much would they know?**

## JOY Burst

# Be Joyful?
## Yes I can, even when...

The perfect man did not come around until I was 31. There were blind dates...a lot of them. I used to tell myself that I was just practicing until the right man came around. I kept reading books about marriage, stayed active in church and hosted a morning radio show at a Christian station.

One day I received a letter thanking me for being the morning announcer. The listener mentioned I had encouraged him through some dark times. His wife had died and left him with two little boys to raise. He wanted to take me out to dinner. I said yes. And later when he wanted to marry me, I said yes! I became a wife and mother all on the same day.

I would like to tell you how easy this all was, except that I cried a lot the first year. I home-schooled one son. My husband went to college at night. At times I felt like a single parent. One day my son saw me reading a book on child rearing. Curiously he asked, "Do you know how to be a parent?" I laughed and thought, "Oh, God, give me wisdom!"

As I reflect on those early years of marriage, I realize my expectations were so unrealistic. I discovered that the best way to begin blending a family was to thank God for them and to keep my sense of humor in this mission field called "family." A wise friend once told me to not measure my success with the children from the immediate results I get. That would come much later when they are adults. Love takes work and is developed with patience, prayer, and time.

I believe a Mother's greatest sphere of influence is with her children and husband! I praise God for immersing me in His grace and His joy that is my sustaining strength!

God's grace is always sufficient!
*Joy Burst Lynn Berna,*
*Ohio*

*For I know the plans I have for you, declares the Lord. Plans to prosper you and not to harm you, plans to give you hope and a future.*
*Jeremiah 29:11*

# Been There, Done That

## ■ Joy Buster

**Who me? I feel helpless. I can't set my DVD player, my answering machine, my cell phone, or fix my computer when it crashes. I couldn't do anything about my father's accident. Talk about feeling helpless! Been there, done that – lots!**

## ■ Joy Booster

Everyone sometimes feels helpless. Is there a situation you would like to change and can't? Have you cried out in anguish "I hate feeling this way"? Find reassurance in God's Word and comfort through your personal relationship with Jesus Christ, as these people did: The woman who hemorrhaged for 12 years, Ruth and Naomi at the death of their spouses, the father of the prodigal son. They would probably agree with you... "Helplessness? Been there, done that!" Rejoice in these words of encouragement,

*Now I take limitations in stride, and with*

35

*good cheer, these limitations that cut me down to size—abuse, accidents, opposition, bad breaks. I just let Christ take over! And so the weaker I get, the stronger I become* (2 Corinthians 12:10 MSG). Even in helplessness, your real Source of joy is with you. ***Grab Joy and Go!***

## ■■■■ Joy Injection

> *Don't panic. I'm with you.*
> *There's no need to fear for I'm your God.*
> *I'll give you strength. I'll help you.*
> *I'll hold you steady, keep a firm grip on you.*
> *That's right. Because I, your God,*
> *have a firm grip on you and I'm not letting go.*
> *I'm telling you, 'Don't panic.*
> *I'm right here to help you.'*
> *Isaiah 41:10, 13 MSG*

## ■■■■ Joy Connection

Jesus, my Savior, hold me snuggly
in your arms,
I praise You for the real joy I find in...
Forgive me for...
Help me to make a difference today by...

# Base your life on God, not circumstances!

## Be Joyful?
### Yes I can, even when...

I felt totally helpless when the call came one late
October rainy night. "We found your dad lying outside
in wet leaves with his wheelchair on top of him. He
fell off a five-foot loading dock but we think he's
okay."

Questions raced through my mind as I drove the
20 miles to the nursing home where dad was recover-
ing from a broken hip. How could he be okay? It was
an hour before they found him. How could he get outside? Did an employee forget to lock the door? Only a
few hours earlier we had joked, laughed, and said
good-night and now this nightmare?

I called the squad upon arrival. The emergency
room workers were amazed that he had no broken
bones, not one! As dad laid there, we talked about the
blessings we could still count even in this tragedy...
someone found him, it was a warm fall night and he
only had minor cuts. Dad was in God's presence!

We treasured those few moments of alertness that
we shared together at the hospital. Only God knew
that he would soon have a light stroke and enter his
final week of life. Our presence was continual with
dad and so was the music of a local Christian radio
station that played numerous times that week, "Angels
Among Us." God in His awesome faithfulness was
reminding us that angels were shielding dad,

37

cushioning his fall and keeping me safe as I raced to be with him at the nursing home.

As I have grown in my faith and trust in the Lord, I have learned that when a person feels totally help-less, it does not mean the situation is hopeless! I've learned that to rejoice in all things does not mean that I must be happy about the crisis, but the fact that God will never abandon me, not for one second. That fact causes me outrageous rejoicing! Look for God's presence in all things, even through the use of His protecting angels!

Nothing is hopeless when God is in it!
*Joy Burst Estella, Maine*

*For he will command his angels concerning you*
*to guard you in all your ways….*
*Psalm 91:11*

# But First...

■■■■ ## Joy Buster

**Be Joyful!**
**Who me? How can I? I never finish**
**anything, and I never have time to talk with**
**friends anymore!**

## Joy Booster

Are you a victim of the "But First" Syndrome? You
begin loading the washer, *but* you remember it is trash
day. You stop and take it out. *But* on the way back in
the house you remember the dry cleaning that was left
in the car. You bring it in. *But* on the way through the
kitchen you remember that meat needs to be thawed
for dinner. *But* then you realize the dirty clothes are
still waiting! *But* then your friend calls and needs to
talk. Are you listening or thinking *but first* I need to
get the laundry started? Unfortunately, many things
rob you from taking time to enjoy fellowship. Sure, if
there is a crisis, you are there. *But* what has happened
to the good old days when friends *made*

*the time* to nourish each other, to laugh and cry, to be silly and serious, and just have fun being together? Do it now! Tomorrow may be too *late*. Be exuberant in uplifting prayers for them. Treasure those Jonathan and David kinds of friendships* that help you make it through the day. So talk with your friends - then ***Grab Joy and Go finish something***.

*1 Samuel 20

## Joy Injection

> *Friends love through all kinds of weather,*
> *and families stick together*
> *in all kinds of trouble.*
> *Proverbs 17:17 MSG*

## Joy Connection

Dear Jesus, my Friend,
I praise You for the real joy I find in...
Forgive me for...
Help me to make a difference today by...


**When I would speak and pray to God by myself
a hundred thousand hindrances at once
intervene before I get at it.
Then the devil can throw all sorts
of reasons for delay into my path.**
Martin Luther

# Can't Sleep?

**▬▬** Joy Buster

**Be Joyful!**
**Who me? Not after I've been awake most of**
**the night! I'm tired and grumpy! I have too**
**many things on my mind.**

**▬▬** Joy Booster

Could this be a sign that you are trying to sustain
yourself rather than trusting God? Use those sleepless
times as an opportunity to talk with God. He's always
ready to listen. God promises that you
can enjoy peaceful sleep--not because
your circumstances will change
during the night, but because
His Spirit will sustain you
through it all and give you
comfort and joy! *Grab that Joy*
*and Go (to sleep)!*

**▬▬** Joy Injection

*I will lie down and sleep in peace,*
*for you alone,*
*O Lord, make me dwell in safety.*
*Psalm 4:8*

41

## Joy Connection

Heavenly Father, my Sustainer,
I praise You for the real joy I find in...
Forgive me for...
Help me to make a difference today by...

**Do you go to bed at night to rest up from the day?
Or, do you go to bed at night so the next day
will be yours to use at its fullest?**

# JOY-Toon

Be GLAD wrapped...
You're never leftover with Jesus.
He makes you like new and keeps you fresh!

# Celebrate,
# You Are a Woman of Worth!

## ▰▰▰ Joy Buster

**Be Joyful!**
**Who me? It's not just a bad hair day but a**
**bad EVERYTHING day! I feel worthless!**

## ▰▰▰ Joy Booster

There may be times when you feel you have no worth.
But remember that's your opinion, not God's! Jesus
always saw the importance and affirmed the value of
people. His disciples sent the noisy little children
away, but Jesus stopped everything and invited them
to come to Him. They weren't a nuisance. They
mattered to Him. The women at the well, Ruth, Sarah,
Hagar – all were valuable to
Him. He gave grace constantly.
There is no unimportant
person in His sight! He
proved that at the cross.
Trust God's opinion of
you, not how you feel at
the moment. Develop a
mind-set that will stop life's
steam roller from flattening

43

your joy as His valuable child. God's grace invites you into His joy-filled presence. It is in this intimate relationship with His Son that your struggle to discover your worth can be transformed into a life of serenity, assurance – and true joy. ***Grab Joy and Go, woman of worth!***

## Joy Injection

*Consider the ravens; They do not sow or reap,*
*they have no storeroom or barn; yet God feeds them.*
*And how much more valuable are you than birds!*
*Luke 12:24*

## Joy Connection

God my Father, whose grace abounds,
I praise You for the real joy I find in...
Forgive me for...
Help me to make a difference today by...

**Joy is knowing God**
**could live anywhere -**
**but He chose your heart.**

# JOY Burst

## Be Joyful?
### Yes I can, even when...

When I first found out that I was losing all my hair, I felt embarrassed. For a woman to lose her hair is not very "socially acceptable." I have Alopecia Universalis, an autoimmune disease causing total hair loss.

One night, I remember waking up from a sound sleep and telling myself, *I can do everything through Him who gives me strength* (Philippians 4:13). I hadn't thought about that pertaining to me until then. Suddenly, I knew I could do all things, if only I would just do it! From that time on, I've held my head up high because God was my source of strength and joy. Whenever I'm feeling frazzled, I read this text because it is posted all around my house. His Word revives my spirit like a vitamin shot!

I know in my peaceful heart that Jesus is walking by my side on this journey of trust and faith. This assurance provides me with a "positive attitude." In fact, that's why my doctor called me at home and asked if I would mentor a young girl going through the devastation of Alopecia. If by my example, I can lead someone who is hurting to Christ, it makes my cross easier to bear. After all, Jesus gave His life for me! Alopecia is only a small price to pay if I can be of use to Him.

I always begin the day by asking God to put someone in front of me who is not handling a situation very well. I hope that I can give them comfort through my witness, to totally trust in God, and know that it is only a test.

My advice to others: Think of others first because this also uplifts you. Buy a good wig. Have a sense of humor when you think about the benefits of Alopecia – you save money from haircuts and you can get in and out of the shower in no time! Peace be to you!

God's everlasting arms will
always embrace you!
*Joy Burst Barbara A. Miller,
Ohio*

*He gives strength to the weary
and increases the power of the weak.*
*Isaiah 40:29*

# Designed for Joy

### Joy Buster
**Be Joyful!**
**Who me? Why should I be joyful?**

### Joy Booster

Is your joy-tank filled up or registering just above empty? Do you struggle to find reasons to be joyful in the routine of life? With the birth of God's Son came joy. The angels announced it to the shepherds. Jesus looked at the cross with joy because He knew what He alone could do for you. His resurrection gift, eternal life for you, should cause you to be a joy burst! Joy is real. It is a gift that God makes available to each and every one of His children. Like the manna God provided for Israel, the supply is unlimited! At the Passover meal, He described the special relationship He would

have with His disciples (this includes you too) if they would abide in Him and His love. He wanted them to know joy to the fullest through a consistent *personal relationship* with Him. When your life is intertwined with His, He will help you walk through every detail in your life! Be jubilant! God designed joy and He designed you...*joy-filled you!* **Grab Joy and Go!**

## Joy Injection

*I have told you this*
*so that my joy may be in you,*
*and that your joy may be complete.*
*John 15:11*

## Joy Connection

Dear Jesus,
I praise You for the real joy I find in...
Forgive me for...
Help me to make a difference today by...

**If you want joy, abandon the pursuit of it and go looking for God instead.**

# Diamonds

▰▰▰ ## Joy Buster

**Be Joyful!**
**Who me? My sparkle and shine are stuck**
**behind a big, dark storm cloud!**

▰▰▰ ## Joy Booster

"When a diamond is placed against a dark background, the darkness makes it seem more brilliant.
And, when the diamond is lifted toward a light, all of
its facets are revealed and allowed to sparkle. A
diamond is pretty all by itself, but putting it against a
black background and lifting it up to the light enhances
its radiance and glory. God setteth in pain the jewel of
His joy." *

True spiritual joy shines
brightest against the darkness
of trials. Life's dark
struggles make Christian
joy more intense and
your heart full of praise
more glorious. Focus on
God's everlasting
presence! Imagine His
loving arms wrapped
around you.

49

Lay your head on His shoulder. Cry floods. Jesus wept too. Then be exuberant with praise for His faithfulness. You have a magnificent God! *Grab Joy and Go!*

* Margaret Clarkson, Grace Grows Best in Winter, William B. Eerdmans Publishing Co., Grand Rapids, MI.

## Joy Injection

> *Commit your way to the Lord;*
> *trust in him and he will do this:*
> *He will make your righteousness*
> *shine like the dawn....*
> *Psalm 37:5-6a*

## Joy Connection

Emmanuel,
I praise You for the real joy I find in...
Forgive me for...
Help me to make a difference today by...

**Happiness is not found**
**at the end of the journey,**
**but experienced along the way.**

# JOY Burst

## Be Joyful?
### Yes I can, even when...

My mother conceived me out of wedlock, but later
married my father. She never wanted me. My father
despised me. I was sexually abused by my father from
16 months old into my teen years. Then the physical
contact stopped, but the lust did not. He demanded that
I wear seductive little outfits and parade in front
of him.

I was neglected by my mother. She didn't know
how to cook, so I was always hungry and in poor
health. She knew what my father was doing to me, but
she did nothing about it, except watch me be humiliat-
ed. Neither parent attended church, but they did allow
me to go to Vacation Bible School when I was five.
That's where I first heard about God's love.

Growing up, I wasn't just afraid, I was terrified!
I had to always be on guard especially at night. I had
no place to go to feel secure, not even to my grand-
mother's because she was mentally ill. It was not until
I went to college and attended a church on campus that
I finally knew God as my refuge.

I was baptized and God's Word came alive in my
life. God was speaking personally to me! His Word
literally became the breath I breathed! *Though you
have made me see troubles, many and bitter, you will
restore my life again; from the depths of the earth you
will again bring me up. You will increase my honor
and comfort me once again* (Psalm 71:20-21).

51

Prayer became part of my life around age twelve. I prayed fervently for God's protection and pleaded not to let anything be wrong with my reproductive organs. I wanted to become a godly mother and raise children to love their Redeemer. Great is His faithfulness! I am blessed with a godly husband and five healthy children.

My life has not been easy, yet I still have reason to rejoice. After all, He did spare me from drug addiction and unwanted pregnancies. God knit me together in my mother's womb. He put me here for a purpose. The Almighty everlasting Father "wants me" and there is no greater honor!

God's grace always protects!
*Joy Burst God's Child,*
*Missouri*

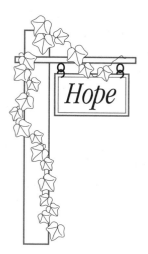

*He who dwells in the*
*shelter of the Most High*
*will rest in the shadow*
*of the Almighty.*
*I will say of the Lord,*
*"He is my refuge and*
*my fortress, my God*
*in whom I trust."*
*Psalm 91:1-2*

# Drifting Values

### ▬▬ Joy Buster

**Be Joyful!**
**Who me? Even when I know I'm**
**compromising my values?**

### ▬▬ Joy Booster

No one is immune to compromising the principles
found in God's Word. Satan encourages you to enjoy
his kind of movies, clothes, friends and to go with the
flow and not uphold your values. Once you take the
first step, Satan urges you to do it again and again.
After all, nothing happened the first time. Without
your realizing it, your lifestyle shifts.

But now, you recognize the shift. You know it's
time to curb the drift. Ask His forgiveness. Anchor
yourself daily in the Word of God so you can hold fast
and refute those who oppose it. The Spirit *will enable*
you to do this through grace. Exhilarating, isn't it?
***Grab Joy and Go!***

### ▬▬ Joy Injection

*If we claim to be without sin, we deceive ourselves*
*and the truth is not in us. If we confess our sins,*
*he is faithful and just and will forgive us our sins*
*and purify us from all unrighteousness.*
*1 John 1:8-9*

## Joy Connection

Dear Heavenly Enabler,
I praise You for the real joy I find in...
Forgive me for...
Help me to make a difference today by...

**The devil too, can quote Scripture.**
**But his use of Scripture is defective.**
**He does not quote it completely**
**but only so much of it as serves his purpose.**
**The rest he silently omits.**

Martin Luther

Keep focused
on Jesus!

54

# Eating My Words

■■■■ Joy Buster

**Be Joyful!**
**Who me? I have tongue whiplash!**

■■■■ Joy Booster

What you say and what you don't say are both important! The right words spoken at the right time can be energizing! But words spoken in haste, can destroy that energy like a bomb! The tongue is like fire; you can neither control nor reverse the damage. Satan uses the tongue to pit people against one another. He causes inflammation of the tongue, triggers gossip, put-downs, complaining, lying, manipulating and exaggerating. Before you speak, ask, "Are my words true, necessary, and kind?" A tongue can leave scars even after an apology. To reduce the damage of your words, pray and ask the Holy Spirit to use what you say to glorify the Lord. To reduce tongue whiplash, Christianize your speech! *Grab Joy and Go use a joy-filled voice.*

55

## Joy Injection

## Joy Connection

Redeemer,
I praise You for the real joy I find in...
Forgive me for...
Help me to make a difference today by...

**Ninety percent of the friction
of daily life is caused
by the wrong tone of voice.**

# Exercise Is for Someone Else

## Joy Buster

**Be Joyful!**
**Who me, exercise? I do it the easy way. I**
**walk to the cupboard, reach for something**
**nutritional, like a chocolate bar, and then**
**walk back to my chair!**

## Joy Booster

Two neighbors were always pulling tricks on each
other. One called the other and said, "I've found the
perfect exercise. Come over, we'll walk around the
block as we finalize the committee plans." Her neighbor arrived in her walking shoes ready to go. "Here,
put this wood block on the floor and we'll walk
around the block together!" Life is too short not to
have fun! Physical exercise takes time, so people put it
off. For the same reason people put off spiritual
exercise too. Does it take too much energy to open
your Bible? Maybe you start to pray, but since you're
out of the habit, you're spiritually short of breath and
you quit early. Have you dropped out of regular
worship? Make this your wake-up call! Exercising
daily with the Lord is *invigorating!* It revitalizes love
and joy! ***Grab Joy and Go exercise.***

57

## Joy Injection

*Whoever is a believer in Christ is a new creation.*
*The old way of living has disappeared.*
*A new way of living has come into existence.*
*2 Corinthians 5:17 GW*

## Joy Connection

Dearest Jesus,

I praise You for the real joy I find in…

Forgive me for…

Help me to make a difference today by…

**Exercise daily,**
**Walk with the Lord.**

# External or Internal

■■■ Joy Buster

**Be Joyful!**
**Who me? What or who can I trust to make**
**me happy?**

■■■ Joy Booster

The dictionary defines *happy* as "pleasure or satisfaction, luck, good fortune" and *joy* as the "source or object of pleasure." You can always be joyful, but you will not always be happy. The difference is in the source. True joy is far deeper than happiness; we can feel joy in spite of our troubles. Happiness is temporary because it is based on external circumstances, but joy is lasting because it is based on God's promises and presence with you. Contemplate His daily presence and you will find contentment. As you understand the future He has for you, you will experience joy overflowing!

59

Remember, that circumstances never change the availability of God's joy to you! Base your life on God, not circumstances – and be exuberant!! ***Grab Joy and Go!***

## Joy Injection

> *You make the path of life known to me.*
> *Complete joy is in your presence.*
> *Pleasures are by your side forever.*
> *Psalm 16:11 GW*

## Joy Connection

Dear Jesus, giver of eternal joy,
I praise You for the real joy I find in...
Forgive me for...
Help me to make a difference today by...

# Joy can be the echo
# of God's life within you.

Duane Pederson

# Focus Problem?

## ▰▰▰ Joy Buster

**Be Joyful!**
**Who Me? I can handle everything! Well**
**maybe a few things. Actually, I don't handle**
**anything very well!**

## ▰▰▰ Joy Booster

Charles Swindoll suggests that life is 10% what you make it and 90% how you take it. Have you ever been like Peter? Nothing could stop him, even walking on the water, when he focused on Christ. But when he let the stressful situation be his focus, splash! The circumstances had not changed but his faith did. *Help!* Jesus reached out to lift Peter up. Peter was where he should have been all the time when he focused on Jesus. Your daily walk is in, on, and through grace!

Knowing this, then why doubt? Do you

really believe He would let you sink in your problems? Your life is never the same once you connect with the real Source of joy! **Grab Joy and Go!**

## Joy Injection

*Peter got down out of the boat,*
*walked on the water and came toward Jesus.*
*But when he saw the wind, he was afraid and,*
*beginning to sink, cried out, "Lord save me!"*
*Immediately Jesus reached out*
*his hand and caught him.*
*"You of little faith," he said, "why did you doubt?"*
*Matthew 14:29-31*

## Joy Connection

Jesus, my Refuge,
I praise You for the real joy I find in...
Forgive me for...
Help me to make a difference today by...

**God grant us all to live as we teach
and to practice what we preach.**
Martin Luther

# Fruit Is Not Invisible

### Joy Buster

**Be Joyful!**
**Who me? Serve fruit? I'd rather serve**
**brownies!**

### Joy Booster

There is no such thing as an invisible grape or apple.
Fruit of the Spirit is visible too! When God says He
wants you to be a fruitful Christian, He wants you to
demonstrate the character of Christ in a very visible
way. Others will be drawn to Him, through the power
of His Spirit, and desire to be connected to the Vine
too, all because of your fruit bearing. Make that
connection strong by praying without ceasing! What
an honor to serve His love and joy through your
uniqueness. *Grab Joy and Go.*

### Joy Injection

*I pray that out of his glorious riches he may strengthen*
*you with power through his Spirit in your inner being,*
*so that Christ may dwell in your heart; through faith.*
*And I pray that you, being rooted and established*
*in love, may have power, ...to grasp how wide and*
*long and high and deep is the love of Christ....*
*Ephesians 3:16-18*

## Joy Connection

Father, Son and Holy Spirit,
I praise You for the joy I find in...
Forgive me for...
Help me to make a difference today by...

**Jesus is the one who helped me smile,
not because of my disability,
but in spite of my disability.**

Joni Eareckson Tada

## JOY-Toon

His Word fills me with joy...

but I don't think it will do the same for you!

# God Can't, So I Can

![joy buster icon] **Joy Buster**

**Be Joyful!**
**Who me? I can't!**

![joy booster icon] **Joy Booster**

Once upon a time, as legend goes, Satan put all his
tools up for sale, except one. He never failed when he
used this specific one in a mind and heart. The tool?
Discouragement and doubt. It worked with Adam and
Eve, and it runs rampant in people today. Praise God
that you can do all the things He asked you to do
because He equips you. Never doubt that miracles
happen! Thank Him for the things He can't do:
change, lie, recall your sins after you have been forgiven, forsake you, go back on His promises, revoke
His gifts, be defeated, do anything contrary to scrip-
tures, ignore your praises, be late, be against you...!
Permeate yourself with positive thinking! Step outside
your comfort zone. God is with you all the way! You
can do it because of His presence! ***Grab Joy and Go!***

![joy injection icon] **Joy Injection**

*The joy you have in the Lord is your strength.*
*Nehemiah 8:10b GW*

## Joy Connection

Father, God, You are a Refuge for all my doubts!
I praise You for the real joy I find in...
Forgive me for...
Help me to make a difference today by...

**Man's way leads to a hopeless end.**
**God's way leads to an endless hope.**

## JOY-Toon

You can have JOY...

...even when you're takin' a lickin'!

# JOY Burst

## Be Joyful?
### Yes I can, even when...

I had no energy. People avoided me because of my health. For 12 years I had tried everything to alleviate my bleeding. Nothing worked. Finally, I heard Jesus was coming my way. I quietly worked my way through the crowd so I could touch Him. No one else noticed me touch the hem of His garment, but He knew. I knew it too. I was healed as only the Great Physician can heal - totally.* My advice to you is, "Don't wait to go to Him." Make it your first priority!  I'm bursting with joy because I know that God's love is authentic. He loves you this way too. We have endless reasons to be a joy burst for our Lord.

* Mark 5

> Go to God first. He is waiting for you.
> *Joy Burst The Hemorrhaging Woman, Heaven*


*My heart trusts in him, and I am helped.*
*My heart leaps for joy and I will give thanks to him...*
*Psalm 28:7*

67

# God's Cheerleader

■■■■ Joy Buster

**Be Joyful!**
**Who Me? Why can't I be a cheerleader, or am I?**

■■■■ Joy Booster

More than anything she wanted to be a cheerleader. *Her plan* was to practice the routines and be chosen. She was devastated when she didn't make the team. She had asked God to make it happen. Why didn't He listen? Did He *have a better plan* for her? As she grew in her relationship with the Lord, and through the work

of the Holy Spirit, she realized that in reality she was a cheerleader promoting the joy of the Lord wherever she went.

Is there something that you want badly right now? Are you willing to rejoice in *all things* even if God takes you on a different journey?

68

When you resolve to allow God to supply *all your needs and refuse to manipulate the circumstances*, you will find contentment! De-stress! Your faithful Father gives you His absolute best when you leave the choice to Him. ***Grab Joy and Go be His cheerleader!***

## Joy Injection

*I will trust in the Lord and not be afraid.*
*Isaiah 12:2*

## Joy Connection

Heavenly Father,
I praise You for the real joy I find in...
Forgive me for...
Help me to make a difference today by...

# The joy is not in the process, but in the outcome.

# God's Presence

### ▰▰▰▰ Joy Buster

**Be Joyful!**
**Who me? Where are you God? I can't take**
**any more of this world's abuse.**

### ▰▰▰▰ Joy Booster

Living under a load of anxiety rapidly depletes your
happiness and robs you of contentment. Satan delights
in feelings of hopelessness. Immerse yourself in faith.
Believe in what cannot be seen. Trust God to use your
situation for eventual good no matter how bad it may
appear. Find hope, comfort, confidence and courage in
God's Word. Remember how Joseph was abused* and
later blessed – and how God's shield of grace covered
Abigail against her husband.** Live one day at a time.
Accept God's provision and daily challenges as you
draw from His strength. Huddle in His refuge. Face
today with confidence. Focus on His presence, then
***Grab Joy and Go!***

\* Genesis 37, 39   \*\* 1 Samuel 25

### ▰▰▰▰ Joy Injection

*Trust in the Lord with all your heart*
*and do not rely on your own understanding.*
*Proverbs 3:5 GW*

## Joy Connection

Father, God, you are a Refuge for all my
doubts!
I praise You for the real joy I find in...
Forgive me for...
Help me to make a difference today by...

## Trust in Him
## rather than speculate about why.

## JOY-Toon

Cart 'em here and
cart 'em there...
so get your
donkey movin'!

# JOY Burst

## Be Joyful?
### Yes I can, even when...

God was talking to me, but I was too stubborn to listen. A vow was made in front of God, and others, that my marriage would last until "death do us part" and that included abuse. I thought that if my husband was treating me that way, I must deserve it.

The belittling and humiliation began soon after we were married and intensified with the arrival of our three children. We moved to another state because he could not keep a job. He said it was all my fault! I prayed God would change him or me; I could always endure for the sake of the children. I would leave no stone unturned to make this happen. I thought no one else ever went through abuse, so I kept quiet.

One day my husband put a 357 magnum to my temple while describing how my remains would look all over the room. Something made me say, "Ok, you coward, do it right now. You'll never get another chance." As I look back, I can see divine intervention because my daughter walked in, and he stopped.

God went beyond patience with my stubbornness. It hit me like a bolt of lightning when I heard my nine year old sobbing because his father was abusing him, and I didn't know. "This is it. God is telling me GET OUT NOW!" Praise God I did because I later learned that my daughters were mentally, physically and sexually being abused too. My husband had so many guns and ammunition in the house that I paid for the divorce by selling them. It is true, that when you are in an abusive relationship you can't see what is going on around you.

As a single Mother with three children and no job, I went to the employment agency and heard, "You have no skills. You are not marketable." I had no money, and the refrigerator was empty. But that day God's love came knocking on my door. It was a young woman with a check for food. How did she know? The Lord knocked again a week later when a Catholic nun came with details about a food surplus place and also directed me to a community college program.

I encourage women in abuse to stop thinking about what "I" can do and trust that God is already opening windows. Just look for them. Don't seek more stones to turn over "on your own." Listen to God's powerful guidance by reading His Word daily. Join Bible study groups to find strength and support. Your name, like mine, is in God's book. Trust Him!

Trust in God's unfailing love!
*Joy Burst Betty, Washington*

*The Lord is a refuge for the oppressed,*
*a stronghold in times of trouble.*
*Those who know your name will trust in you,*
*for you, Lord, have never forsaken those who seek you.*
*Psalm 9:9-10*

# Gray Hair

## Joy Buster

**Be Joyful!**
**Who me? I'm getting gray hair! What will**
**people think? I feel so old. This doesn't**
**make me happy!**

## Joy Booster

God's Word does not say He will stop loving you if
you have a few new, or even *all* gray hair. Have you
ever read an obituary that stated the cause of death as
gray hair? If the world wouldn't make a big deal about
the color of hair, would you? Every season of life has
its own beauty and special joy. Accept yourself and
others as God does! You can have gray hair and
be a vessel of Christ's joy at the same time!
*Grab Joy and Go!*

75

## Joy Injection

*Gray hair is a crown of splendor;*
*it is attained by a righteous life.*
*Proverbs 16:31*

*Even when you're old, I'll take care of you.*
*Even when your hair turns gray, I'll support you.*
*I made you and will continue to care for you.*
*I'll support you and save you.*
*Isaiah 46:4 GW*

## Joy Connection

Heavenly Father, my personal designer,
I praise You for the real joy I find in...
Forgive me for...
Help me to make a difference today by...

**God's promises are a bottomless**
**reservoir of joy**
**which can be drawn from,**
**even with gray hair.**

# Happy Birthday to Me

### ▰▰▰ Joy Buster

**Be Joyful!**
**Who me? It's my birthday, again!**

### ▰▰▰ Joy Booster

Do you dread having another birthday? Delete the doom-and-gloom about adding another number to your age. Insert a joyous attitude. There *is* reason to celebrate with outburst of praise for God's blessings this past year. Think about this: How many times has God forgiven you? Has He kept you safe? Has He provided water to drink and ample food to eat? Can you blink, cough, sneeze, swallow, and laugh? Wow, think of all the things taken for granted this past year! Faithful is your God! Whatever the future holds you can handle it because your God does not change. Neither does His promise to guide your footsteps as long as you walk with Him! Go ahead, celebrate! Eat cake and all your

favorite foods. Laugh and be silly with friends. You are never too old to have fun, especially when you are God's child! ***Grab Joy and Go blow out the candles!***

## Joy Injection

*Before I was born the Lord called me,*
*from my birth He has made mention of my name.*
*Isaiah 49:1b*

## Joy Connection

Awesome God,
I praise You for the real joy I find in...
Forgive me for...
Help me to make a difference today by...

# Don't count how many years you've spent, Just count the good you've done!

# Help, I'm a Mother

## Joy Buster

**Be Joyful!**
**Who me? I'm a Mother. There are times**
**when I wish I could resign.**

## Joy Booster

Colic, diapers and 2 a.m. feedings can surely drain
your energy! So can toddler temper tantrums – and
teenage curfews! As a mother, it isn't easy to be the
glue that holds the family together. You set the mood
of the day, and if mom's not happy, it affects everyone.
But you don't need to bear the burden alone. Proceed
with confidence as the Holy Spirit guides you. Wrap
yourself in the assurance of Christ's love, and don't
give up the task that God has given you. He planned
your entire life and it includes this part of the journey

too. Drink daily from
God's Word, your
personal
instruction
manual for
motherhood!
Offer praise
because
your godly
witness can
affect many

79

generations. Doubt it? Just watch and listen to your children and you'll see yourself. They are like sponges soaking up whatever you are modeling. God used an amateur to build the ark, but trained professionals built the Titanic. His on-the-job training will carry you through! Rejoice! You make a difference in the word *Mother*! ***Grab Joy and Go!***

## Joy Injection

*And let the loveliness of our Lord, our God, rest on us,*
*confirming the work that we do.*
*Oh, yes. Affirm the work that we do!*
*Psalm 90:17 MSG*

## Joy Connection

Father, You are my Fortress,
I praise You for the real joy I find in...
Forgive me for...
Help me to make a difference today by...

**God has entrusted us**
**with family and friends**
**and charged us with living in a way**
**that helps them draw closer to Him.**

Emilie Barnes

# Hope In a Jar

## Joy Buster

**Be Joyful!**
**Who me? No matter what I do I can't look like the magazine covers tell me I'm supposed to.**

## Joy Booster

Have you ever caught yourself reading magazine covers as you check out at the grocery store? "New Fashions"... "The Flawless Look"... "New Beauty Tips" are articles women devour to help them become new and improved. Who dreams up these impossible standards? Are they coming from a company wanting to sell hope in a jar, or box, or brand name? Real beauty comes from the heart. Not even blemishes or the shape of your body can mask the beauty of the Lord living in your heart! His joy-glow can never be hidden! Look at yourself through Christ's eyes. He loves you just as you are! He *proved* it through His

 Son's death for your sins! *Nothing* should take that joy from your heart! *Grab Joy and Go glow!*

81

## Joy Injection

## Joy Connection

Dear Awesome Creator,
I praise You for the real joy I find in...
Forgive me for...
Help me to make a difference today by...

**The great
beautifier
is a
contented heart
and a
happy outlook.**

# Hot Fudge Sundae and a Diet Coke

## ▰ Joy Buster

**Be Joyful!**
**Who me? Even when I'm like a vacuum cleaner around food?**

## ▰ Joy Booster

Many people have a difficult time understanding others when they say, "I can't eat when I am upset." To most people that is a foreign concept! We comfort ourselves while trying to forget our stress. Then the battle of the voices begins: "You know you shouldn't have eaten that!" "Go ahead, it feels good, have more!" Has food ever solved even one of our problems? Or, did it just delay facing the situation? Now, the problem still exists and there are extra pounds too! It takes approximately 21 days to form a habit. Begin today. Pray for strength. Start turning to the Lord *first* instead of food or drinks that offer false comfort. We can *be confident* that God

will help us work through our problems. His authentic Comfort will not add pounds but make us feel lighter! Our strength is in the joy of the Lord! Forget instant happiness. ***Grab Joy and Go for the real thing!***

## Joy Injection

*For our struggle is not against flesh and blood,*
*but against the rulers, against the authorities,*
*against the powers of this dark world*
*and against the spiritual forces of evil*
*in the heavenly realms.*
*Therefore put on the full armor of God....*
*Ephesians 6:12-13a*

## Joy Connection

Father, You are the Source of my strength,
I praise You for the real joy I find in...
Forgive me for...
Help me to make a difference today by...

**Food and drink
can be very pleasurable
but only goodness, peace, and joy
can satisfy the soul.**

Fun Nun

# Hurry Up!

## Joy Buster

**Be Joyful!**
**Who me? Maybe I could if my kids would**
**ever stop dawdling!**

## Joy Booster

Do your children *always* listen and do everything you
ask them to do the first time? It is amazing how kids
can perfect the art of selective hearing, even at a
young age! Likewise, parents perfect the words
"NOW" or "If you don't...I'm going to..." How
would you celebrate if your children would always
obey? Have you ever thought about how your
Heavenly Father feels when He asks you to be still,
*listen, follow and obey Him?* You can jump for joy (or
tap your toes) because your Heavenly Father never
threatens when you use selective listening to His
parental Word! God is forgiving – are you? Live in
obedience to your Father. Give your children an
example to follow. ***Grab Joy and Go practice***
***listening!***

## Joy Injection

*I will hasten and not delay to obey your commands.*
*Psalm 119:60*

## Joy Connection

Perfect Father, my model,
I praise You for the real joy I find in...
Forgive me for...
Help me to make a difference today by...

## God has your whole life in mind when He directs you.

## JOY-Toon

# I Blew It and I Knew It

## Joy Buster

**Be Joyful!**
**Who Me? How can I be joyful when I feel**
**like a total failure? I blew it and I knew it.**
**In fact, I'm so embarrassed I wonder why I**
**was ever born?**

## Joy Booster

You are God's idea! Your life is no accident! At the
time of conception there are over five million sperm
and only one egg. God *intended* for you to be born!
Life is like a yo-yo with ups and downs, failures and
successes. King David blew it. He knew it.* Yet he
trusted God and rejoiced in His forgiveness.

You are never a failure in God's
redeeming eyes. The joy of His
presence will be with you
always... even when
you blow it! *Grab Joy
and Go!*

* 2 Samuel 11

87

## Joy Injection

*Your eyes saw my unformed body.*
*All the days ordained for me were written*
*in your book before one of them came to be.*
*Psalm 139:16*

## Joy Connection

Dear Almighty Creator,
I praise You for the real joy I find in...
Forgive me for...
Help me to make a difference today by...

# God won't give up on you.
# Don't give up on God.

# I'm Here to Help

## Joy Buster

**Be Joyful!**
**Who me? I'll go help her but it better not**
**take long!**

## Joy Booster

It's said that when a goose gets sick, wounded or shot down, two geese drop out of flying formation and follow it down to help and protect it. They stay with it until it dies or is able to fly again. Then, they launch out with another formation or catch up with the flock. *It is more important to let another know how much you care than how much you know!* Your encouraging

89

words in difficult times, as well as good times, will not only give others a joy-boost but you too! That is joy doubled! Be a joy-giver wherever you go!
***Grab Joy and Go!***

## Joy Injection

*I hope to visit and talk things over with you personally.*
*Then we will be completely filled with joy.*
*2 John 1:12b GW*

## Joy Connection

Heavenly Enabler,
I praise You for the real joy I find in...
Forgive me for...
Help me to make a difference today by...

# Burdens are not heavy when everybody lifts.

# JOY Burst

## Be Joyful?
### Yes I can, even when...

I've heard that if we live long enough we are all "once
an adult but twice a child." When I became a "parent"
to my elderly father I clearly understood being part of
the "sandwich generation."

Even though my Dad was 93 and had typical
health ailments, he insisted he could live alone.
Whenever I suggested he move closer to me, he ended
the discussion! His church family brought him food
and friendship. The neighbors helped us contact him
when he would leave his hearing aid out and was
unable to hear the phone, no matter how long or often
I let it ring!

One morning he called and said, "I thought you
ought to know I didn't sleep a bit last night." I recognized this as a cry for help. I had been taught to
"Honor thy father." which had come to mean, "Don't
go against his will." However, I knew it was time
to act. Within the week he was in an assisted living
facility near my house. He was hurt and angry. The
intensity of his bitterness was clear when he said, "I
hope you live to be 93 and someone takes you out of
your home."

I knew that he needed to be with others of his
generation. Also, he needed balanced meals to replace
the McDonald's® specials and bread with jelly that had
become his routine. He was no longer capable of

driving, because of severe loss of hearing, exemplified one morning when he was oblivious to blaring fire engines. But knowing all this didn't remove the hurt look on his face. However, one time when I stopped for my daily visit he said, "Is it that time already?" God knew I needed that encouragement!

Now I see the Master's plan more clearly: The retirement home that wasn't there a few years earlier, the people who joyfully welcomed him, the great grandchildren he could enjoy, and the change in my job that allowed me to worship with him on Sunday. He never wanted to miss church! Daddy was never happier than when he could tell a story and have someone's undivided attention. How like our heavenly Father who wants our attention too.

Listen carefully to what aging parents say. The Holy Spirit will guide your decisions. Always have hope! Look for God's blessings in disguise - they're there! Continue to pray that the Lord will give you wisdom and understanding because you too may become a "child twice!"

The JOY of the Lord was my strength!
*Joy Burst Shirley Braddock, Ohio*

*Guide me in your truth*
*and teach me,*
*for you are God my Savior,*
*and my hope is in you*
*all day long.*
*Psalm 25:5*

# Identity Crisis

## ▰▰▰ Joy Buster

**Be Joyful!**
**Who me? I'm a woman, wife, mother,**
**grandmother, employee, volunteer,**
**friend....There are days I wonder who I**
**really am!**

## ▰▰▰ Joy Booster

Imagine that a special delivery letter just arrived that could change your life forever. But first, you must respond to this request: Describe in detail who you are. You fill out the information about your education, career, church, and give glowing references. You include your best photo – definitely not a copy of your passport or drivers license photos!

Mission accomplished. In a few days the packet is returned, marked "Application Incomplete. Your information tells about your achievements, performance, and what you look like, but not who you are."*

In life we may have many jobs, even several

careers and dozens of responsibilities. But our *real identity* comes from being God's child, a member of God's family, personally related to Christ and redeemed by Him. Exude joy because of whose you are! Your perception of this personal relationship will determine how you deal with daily life, establish priorities and treat others. Seeing yourself through God's eyes is the core to rejoicing in your identity. ***Grab Joy and Go!***

*Story source unknown

## Joy Injection

> *If we live, we honor the Lord,*
> *and if we die, we honor the Lord.*
> *So whether we live or die, we belong to the Lord.*
> *Romans 14:8 GW*

## Joy Connection

Almighty God,
I praise You for the real joy I find in...
Forgive me for...
Help me to make a difference today by...

**Our gratitude to God should be as regular as our beating heart.**

# If Only

## Joy Buster

**Be Joyful!**
**Who me? When it is summer, I want winter.**
**When I was a child, I wanted to be an adult.**
**When I was 39, I wanted to be 29. If only**
**things could be perfect!**

## Joy Booster

If you know someone who is looking for the perfect
life, warn them that they're in for a big surprise here
on planet earth. Just think, though - *everything* will be
perfect in heaven! Can you even imagine what total
perfection would be like? That's an overwhelming
thought! Being entrenched in what life *ought* to be
often leads to stress and bitterness. Wanting change is
wonderful, if it is for the right reason
at the right time. Wanting change
at the wrong time causes us to
miss out on
enjoying today
by living in the
future. God's
mercies are new
every morning.
Eagerly anticipate
His plans for

your day. Enjoy the sunshine along with the rain. After all, the grass needs to drink too. Each season in life has its own kind of unique blessings. Say good-by to Satan's negative thoughts. With gladness greet the Holy Spirit, who will empower you to be a glow-in-the-dark Christian - that's having a Christ-like attitude in this doom-and-gloom world! Life is *too short* not to live intentionally! Spread mega doses of heaven-brought joy! ***Grab Joy and Go see what your awesome God has planned for you today!***

## Joy Injection

*Show me your ways, O Lord, teach me your paths;*
*guide me in your truth and teach me,*
*for you are God my Savior,*
*and my hope is in you all day long.*
*Psalm 25:4-5*

## Joy Connection

Lead me today, Lord.
I praise You for the real joy I find in...
Forgive me for...
Help me to make a difference today by...

# There are 365 days in a year, but there is only one we should be concerned about and that is today.

# Is Anything Really Free?

## ■ Joy Buster

**Be Joyful!**
**Who me? When everything costs so much?**
**Will there ever be an end to higher prices?**

## ■ Joy Booster

What would your ancestors say about the price you pay for bread or stamps or gas? The reality in this world is that everything keeps costing more. However, as God's child, there is one cost that you can celebrate and rejoice. Jesus paid for you to have the *free gift* of eternal life. No strings attached. Believe this! Humbly

receive it. This truth sets you free to explode with joy! ***Grab Joy and Go!***

Believe:
• Jesus died on the cross for your sins.
• He rose from the dead.
• You will have eternal life.

## Joy Injection

*For God so loved the world that he gave his one
and only Son, that whoever believes in him
should not perish but have eternal life.*
*John 3:16*

## Joy Connection

Dear Personal Savior,
I praise You for the real joy I find in...
Forgive me for...
Help me to make a difference today by...

# If you died today
# would you go to heaven?

# Is It Morning Already?

## Joy Buster

**Be joyful!**
**Who me? When the alarm goes off much too early and I'm not ready to get up?**

## Joy Booster

Which do you say when it's time to get up: "Good Morning Lord" or "I don't do mornings!" God has given you a new day to be on a mission for Him. In all the earth no one else will have a day exactly like yours. No matter what happens, *focus* on God's goodness. You can be a difference maker for Him even in the tiniest details. This includes trying to find matching socks, putting them back on a young child for the umpteenth time or washing them for a shut-in. Bask in the thought that Jesus is right there beside you filling you with His joy even in the mundane things. Glisten with gladness in all that you do in His name. ***Grab Joy and Go!***

99

## Joy Injection

*This is the day the Lord has made;*
*let us rejoice and be glad in it.*
*Psalm 118:24*

## Joy Connection

Lord of real joy,
I praise You for the real joy I find in...
Forgive me for...
Help me to make a difference today by...

**Will what you do today
make a difference five years from now,
one year from now?**

# It Hurts So Much

## ■ Joy Buster

**Be Joyful!**
**Who me? I can not think about joy at a time**
**like this. My pain is too deep.**

## ■ Joy Booster

Many Christians are like a man who was walking
along the road carrying a heavy load over his shoul-
ders. A tractor pulling a wagon stopped to offer him a
ride. He joyfully accepted. But when seated he kept
holding his heavy load. "Why don't you lay down
your burden?" asked the driver. "Oh!" replied the man,
"I feel that it is almost too much to ask you to carry
me, and I could not think of letting you carry my
burden too." *

When the prognosis is not good for a son, daughter, spouse or another loved one and you feel like you
aren't even strong enough to pray, be confident that
the Spirit will intercede for you. *When you are weak-
est, He is strongest!* God knows the pain you are going
through. He went to Gethsemane and Calvary. He can
personally identify with your agony. He knows how
hopeless you feel. He knows the churning in the pit of
your stomach. Wrap yourself in the refuge of His comforting arms. Rely on all that you have learned about
Him. His Spirit will enable you to endure and deal

101

with daily life while you feel as though your heart is dying. Inhale His love and His promise to be with you *always*. Exhale *hope* that will lead to contentment because you are in God's presence. No, you aren't walking on Happy Lane right now. But, you are encompassed in eternal joy. ***Grab Joy and Go cry your heart out.***

*Hannah Whitall Smith

## Joy Injection

*Give ear to my words, O Lord, consider my sighing. Listen to my cry for help,... In the morning, O Lord, you hear my voice; in the morning I lay my requests before you and wait in expectation.*
*Psalm 5:1-3*

## Joy Connection

Jesus, Jesus, how I desperately need You!
I praise You for the real joy I find in...
Forgive me for...
Help me to make a difference today by...

**God still draws near to us in the ordinary, everyday experiences and places. He comes in surprising ways.**
Henry Gariepy

# JOY Burst

## Be Joyful?
### Yes I can, even when...

People would ask me, "How can you just go on?" referring to the sudden death of my daughter and mother of two young children. What else can you do? Grieving endlessly would not bring her back. Life would go on. Christ had sustained me in the past; therefore I could face tomorrow trusting in His plan. In every aspect, parents always wish the best for their children, and ultimately eternal life. Yet, in our human-ness, we want to keep them with us here forever.

One thing certain about life is that change is inevitable. Unfortunately when change is so rampant, terror and hopelessness become prevalent. This change in our family unit has given me the chance to reflect on this...*Always be prepared to give an answer to everyone who asks you to give the reason for the hope that you have* (1 Peter 3:15).

God used this change in my life, to help me become much more tolerant with people who are grieving. I now find myself witnessing on a daily basis, whenever I can. There have been numerous seats next to me on the airplane that lent to the occasion just admirably. You know, the Lord puts you in those positions. God has used me to minister to other women who have lost children and I praise Him for this opportunity. It is easy to speak of the peace, strength and joy that I have found in the Lord because my faith continues to grow!

The most meaningful thing anyone ever told me was that I would feel the closest to my daughter every time I took communion. It's true, I never celebrate communion without thinking of her as we praise God "…with all the company of Heaven."

I encourage you to take the opportunity to witness your love for the Lord. Yes, even in changing circumstances, the joy of the Lord will be with you!

God is always at work in your life!
*Joy Burst Virginia Von Seggern, Nebraska*

*May the God of hope fill you with all joy and peace*
*as you trust in Him*
*so that you may overflow with hope*
*by the power of the Holy Spirit.*
*Romans 15:13*

# It Is All In Your Point of View

### Joy Buster

**Be Joyful!**
**Who me? Cheer up someone else,**
**the way I feel?**

### Joy Booster

Two men, both seriously ill, occupied the same hospital room. One man was allowed to sit up in his bed for an hour each afternoon. The other man had to stay flat on his back. They talked about their families and jobs. Every afternoon when the man in the bed by the window could sit up, he would pass the time by describing in exquisite detail all the things he could see outside the window: a park with ducks, old trees, playgrounds, and an ice cream stand. Days and weeks passed. One morning, the nurse found the lifeless body of the man by the window. The other man asked if he could be moved next to the window. He discovered it faced a blank wall. "What compelled his roommate to describe all those things?" he asked. The nurse then told him that the man was blind and perhaps

105

he just wanted to encourage you.*

There is great joy in making others happy *despite* your own situation. So, look past your troubles and enjoy the gift of today! Give yourself a joy boost as you discover the opportunities this day offers to encourage a friend, a neighbor, a co-worker, a relative. ***Grab that Joy and Go!***

*Story source unknown

## Joy Injection

> *Encourage each other every day*
> *while you have the opportunity.*
> *Hebrews 3:13a GW*

## Joy Connection

Dear Jesus,
I praise You for the real joy I find in...
Forgive me for...
Help me to make a difference today by...

# The smallest good deed is better than the greatest intention.

# It's Hot in Here!

## ■■■ Joy Buster

**Be Joyful!**
**Who me? I'm hot and this is not the typical hot flash!**

## ■■■ Joy Booster

Fire turns clay into pottery. Time in the kiln is essential for endurance. The cause for cracking has nothing to do with the thickness of the vessel. It is from the abrupt change in temperature. Job survived his time in the kiln. He wasn't happy, but he was never without the presence of the Lord. Job found a new intimacy with God; one that he could never have known without suffering. When you are in the kiln, super-glue yourself to God's promises that He will never leave you, nor will the fire consume you. That is assurance! That's energizing! No person who has

107

ever endured the testing will ever be the same. Fire brings forth vessels of endurance, supreme value, beauty and strength from the ashes of adversity. Will you choose to walk on Joy Lane or Misery Road? **_Grab Joy and Go!_**

## ███ Joy Injection

*Fear not, for I have redeemed you;*
*I have summoned you by name; you are mine.*
*When you pass through the waters, I will be with you;*
*and when you pass through the rivers,*
*they will not sweep over you.*
*When you walk through the fire,*
*you will not be burned;*
*the flames will not set you ablaze.*
*Do not be afraid, for I am with you.*
*Isaiah 43:1b-2, 5*

## ███ Joy Connection

Father, My Strength and Refuge,
I praise You for the real joy I find in...
Forgive me for...
Help me to make a difference today by...

# Christians have hope and hope can be joy in disguise.

# Joy at Any Age!

## Joy Buster
**Be Joyful!**
**Who me? How can I find joy at my age?**

## Joy Booster

Aging is inevitable even though magazines offer tips on how to "look 10 years younger" and "disguise the aging process." Could it be that what we really dislike is what happens to us in the changing seasons of life? Our energy level isn't what it used to be. There are new health problems. The thought of the loss of loved ones is overwhelming! Celebrate what Scripture says about aging. Glisten with gladness because God looks at aging quite differently than we do. He doesn't camouflage the old, He restores! God assures us there will never come a time when we no longer have a purpose. Mary was a teenager when Jesus was born. As a young girl, Miriam watched baby Moses in a basket. Years later she crossed the Red Sea with him and led the women in a joy-filled praise dance. Sarah was past menopause (and then some!) when Isaac was born! God has no age limits. Whether you are living at home or in a nursing home, His strength is made perfect in your weakness. Be a-dazzle, *yes even at your age*, about your guarantee of eternal life. No age limits there either! You are exactly the age God wants you to be right now! Make peace with this because you trust His grace. ***Grab Joy and Go enjoy your day!***

## Joy Injection

*Do not lose heart.*
*Though outwardly we are wasting away,*
*yet inwardly we are being renewed day by day.*
*2 Corinthians 4:16*

## Joy Connection

Dearest Jesus, I am nothing without You,
I praise You for the real joy I find in...
Forgive me for...
Help me to make a difference today by...

**The God of the ages is also the God of the aging!**

# Joy Glasses

Joy Buster
**Be Joyful!**
**Who me? Where is God when I need Him?**

Joy Booster

A soldier was trying to find a refuge to escape from his enemies. As he darted through the hillsides, he saw a cave and entered. The private listened intently and heard the footsteps of his enemy approaching. Trying to silence his breathing, he watched a spider spin a web across the cave opening. Then he heard the enemy stop at the cave, examine the entry and shout, "He can't be in here or this spider's web would be broken."*

Coincidence or God's plans? From our perspective, a situation may look hopeless. But, to God, it is all part of the perfect plan He has choreographed for our lives. Scripture is absolutely clear that nothing occurs, not one bump on life's road, beyond the reach of God's power. When we come to know the truth of God's Word and to entrust our lives to our Savior,

111

then we begin to see our lives in a whole new perspective. His Spirit daily renews you for the challenges and opportunities that are part of your life here on earth. His Spirit enables you to joyfully follow His example and fix your eyes, not on what is seen—the temporary— but on what is unseen: the eternal. Be assured of Jesus' love! Then joyfully anticipate His blessings in disguise. His joy-Light is shining for you! *Grab Joy and Go look for His fingerprints in your day!*

*Story Source Unknown

## Joy Injection

*For I know the plans I have for you, declares the Lord,*
*plans to prosper you and not to harm you,*
*plans to give you hope and a future.*
*Jeremiah 29:11*

## Joy Connection

Almighty Protector,
I praise You for the real joy I find in...
Forgive me for...
Help me to make a difference today by...

**As we contemplate His daily presence,**
**we will find contentment.**
**Don't base your life on circumstances,**
**but on God.**

# JOY Burst

## Be Joyful?
### Yes I can, even when...

Like Job, my life went from muck to a miracle too. In fact, my friends call me "Miracle Mary"!

With no warning the panic attacks began. The emergency room nurses confirmed that my blood pressure was extremely high. What they didn't know was how low my spirit was. After a week of tests in the hospital, a doctor suggested my son admit me to the psychiatric ward where I stayed for one month.

I went for counseling and anger management. Stress? Anger? Could this have come from: My husband, the church president, who ran away with a friend? Years of knowing that my mother left me in a basket on a doorstep? Incest from one of my adoptive mother's husbands?

Only God knew how abandoned and full of shame I felt. I didn't want to see anyone, ever! He knew I was drowning in the deepest pit in hell. But God also knew the magnificent miracle He had planned for my life!

At God's perfect timing, I found a Christian counselor who adjusted my medication, helped me understand that this was an illness - not a disease, and talked to me about God's Word. I'd gone to church for years, but now, I fully understood the depth of God's unfailing love!

I submitted my worry, my negative attitude, and my lack of confidence to my Savior. He would never abandon me, ever! The contentment I had searched for was within me. God enabled me to do things I'd never imagined. There is tremendous joy in being a hospital volunteer and offering compassion to the hurting! This detour through life restored and energized me!

Whenever you are in life's pits, never give up. Have hope! Trust that God created you for a purpose that only you could fulfill! Never forget that even if you were the only person on earth, Jesus would still have died for your sins. His love is that encompassing!

> God never left me!
> *Joy Burst Miracle Mary,*
> *Florida*

*You will surely forget your trouble,*
*recalling it only as waters gone by.*
*Life will be brighter than noonday,*
*and darkness will become like morning.*
*You will be secure, because there is hope; you will*
*look about you and take your rest in safety.*
*Job 11:16-18*

# Joy-A-Tude, Why Me?

## ▰ Joy Buster

**Be Joyful!**
**Who me? All I want to know is, "Why me?"**

## ▰ Joy Booster

Joseph might have cried out, "Why, God? What good could ever come of my being thrown into this pit?" Mary could have questioned, "Are You sure You want me to have a child, Lord?" You might be asking, "Why am I the one with this illness…in this leadership role…with this family conflict…?" In the midst of the darkest cloud, focus on Sonshine. When you feel over-whelmed, there is reason to send up joy fireworks because it is the size of your God, not the size of your obstacle that counts. God did not bring Noah into the middle of the flood only to forget about him! It is not the circumstances of life that are most important, but your *attitude* toward them and how you permit them to affect you. What He allowed to come into your life yesterday has helped prepare you for today, and what today

115

brings will equip you better for tomorrow. Let God's "I Am" drown out your weak "I can't!" The fact is, you can always find joy in His presence. Walk at His pace while He stretches your faith! ***Grab Joy and Go!***

## Joy Injection

*I can do everything through him*
*who gives me strength.*
*Philippians 4:13*

*...God is faithful; he will not let you be tempted*
*beyond what you can bear.*
*1 Corinthians 10:13*

*God will meet all your needs....*
*Philippians 4:19*

## Joy Connection

Almighty God, My Refuge,
I praise You for the real joy I find in...
Forgive me for...
Help me to make a difference today by...

# Your greatest opportunities
# are cleverly disguised
# as insurmountable problems!

# JOY Burst

## Be Joyful?
### Yes I can, even when...

December 3, 1997, was just an ordinary day. I went for my annual mammogram. When the radiologist called for another picture, I still wasn't overly anxious. But when she came to talk to me, I knew that it was serious. The subsequent biopsy confirmed a fast growing kind of breast cancer.

I felt devastated! I began to think that I would not see my grandchildren grow up. My husband of 41 years would be left alone. My Pastor said to me, "Just remember that having cancer is not a death sentence." This triggered me to think in a more positive way. I began looking at my family, and the world, with new eyes.

I have always had a strong faith but I still questioned, "Why me?" Then, the day before surgery during my devotional time, I suddenly began to think, "Why not me? I'm no different from anyone else. God doesn't love me more." I finally submitted to God. I knew that however things turned out, I would be a winner! The incredible peace that swept over me was indescribable. From that moment on I felt assured that everything would be all right. I was not afraid.

During my prayer time at the hospital I said, "OK, God, everything is supposed to work together for good for those who love You and are called according to Your purpose. What is the good in my cancer?"

I did not wait long for the answer. A young nurse came in my room, saw my devotional books, and began to ask questions. As we talked about God and how He works in our lives, I learned she had a life-affecting decision to make. She seemed encouraged by our talk and thanked me for listening and sharing my faith.

God is faithful to His promises! Trusting the presence of the Lord in my life, has been my strength in both my recovery, remission, and my witnessing! His promises are for you too!

God gives peace beyond our understanding!
*Joy Burst Libbie Johnson, Ohio*

*I am with you always, to the very end of the age.*
*Matthew 28:20*

# Joyercise*

## ■ Joy Buster

**Be Joyful!**
**Who me? How can I love her, after what she did to me?**

## ■ Joy Booster

To Joyercise* is to put God's love into action! It's amazing how your Spirit is willing but your sinful flesh gets in the way when it means being totally unselfish! To Joyercise means to direct God's love outward, toward others, not inward toward yourself. To do that is challenging because Satan works over-time. However, it is possible to practice this love only if God helps you set aside your own desires and instincts, so that you can give love while expecting nothing in return. Write your name on the lines.

___'s (your name) love is patient. ___ love is kind.

___love does not envy.

___ love does not boast, it is not proud

___ love is not rude, it is not self-seeking

___ love is not easily angered

___ love keeps no record of wrongs

___ love does not delight in evil but rejoices in truth

___ love always protects, always trusts, always hopes, always perseveres – because… God's love never fails!

119

Rejoice in the fact that even when you fail to Joyercise, He still loves you! ***Grab Joy and Go!***

## Joy Injection

*Be joyful always; pray continually;*
*give thanks in all circumstances,*
*for this is God's will for you in Christ Jesus.*
*1 Thessalonians 5:16-18*

## Joy Connection

O Lord, Who filled my heart with love,
I praise You for the real joy I find in...
Forgive me for...
Help me to make a difference today by...

**Joyercise Tip:** Buy yourself and your grandchild (or another young friend) a journal. Share names of people to pray for, reasons to offer praise, and how you felt God's presence in your day!!

*Joyercise, Word/Meaning by Annetta E. Dellinger

# The key to life
# is how you deal with Plan B.

# Kaleidoscope Life

**Be Joyful!**

**Who me? Will anything good ever come out of the pieces of my life?**

## ■■■■ Joy Booster

When you think back through all you did in one day, have you ever wondered how all those things fit together and give meaning to life? Making phone calls, unloading sacks of groceries, hemming pants, peeling potatoes, fixing refreshments for a meeting, listening to the dreams and depressions of a family member, and taking meals to your parents are all little fragments in the big picture of your life. Life is like a kaleidoscope. You are the cylinder. The bits and pieces of broken glass (the circumstances in your day) remain just that until they are held up to the light (Son Light). It is while the kaleidoscope is in God's *sustaining* hands that the jagged, disjointed pieces become

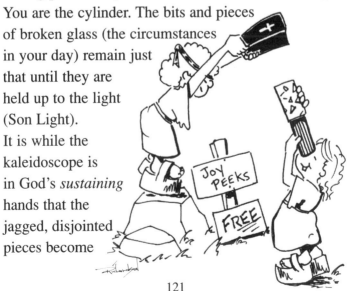

121

part of His magnificent design for your *life*. Through faith, these all add up, and the mundane does have purpose! Now, in each insignificant piece, there is beauty!* Awesome beauty! Shout for joy to the Lord and enjoy each day to the fullest! ***Grab Joy and Go!***

Story is Author's Paraphrase from ideas in: <u>When God Shines Through</u>, Claire Cloninger, Word Publishing

## Joy Injection

> *We know that all things work together*
> *for the good of those who love God—*
> *those whom he has called according to his plan.*
> Romans 8:28 GW

## Joy Connection

Father, How magnificent is your name in all the earth,
I praise You for the real joy I find in...
Forgive me for...
Help me to make a difference today by...

# Enjoy the scenery along the detour. God is with you.

# JOY Burst

## Be Joyful?
### Yes I can, even when...

Everyone has problems or a crisis that creeps into their lives. Ours crept in quietly and had the victim and the caregivers in its web of darkness before we even realized what had happened. My husband's depression came on slowly so we didn't recognize it at first, but between October and January we realized that there was no joy in his life anymore. He would stay in bed through much of the day, wouldn't talk except to give short answers to questions, and had no desire to even eat. He was in his own world of darkness. Suicidal feelings of hopelessness sent him to the hospital.

The caregivers, his family, had to take on the job of running the farm and the myriad of other tasks that we never had to think about before. Our joy was dwindling, too. We didn't understand the WHY of the situation. There was joy all around us; why couldn't he see it? Why couldn't he just take a deep breath and get up and do a few small tasks of the day?

The weeks dragged into months and then into years. We learned that his problem was a chemical imbalance and only through medication could he get better. But it took months and months and months to balance it correctly. In the meantime, the caregivers were exhausted and often emotionally drained, but through prayer and kind Christian friends we held together.

God and I talked a lot during those hard times. I couldn't burden the children any more than they already were, so it was God and I talking together every day. He sustained me and sometimes carried me. When I was so overwhelmed that I couldn't pray, I knew the Holy Spirit carried my burden to our Lord. *The Spirit helps us in our weakness. We do not know what we ought to pray for, but the Spirit himself intercedes for us with groans that words cannot express.* (Romans 8:26)

Through God's grace, we made it! We are a joyful family praising God for the blessings given to us. The joy of our rough journey comes from knowing the love and strength of our family and Christian friends – and our Lord! God's love was and is always there for us. How wonderful!

God was my strength and refuge!
*Joy Burst God's Child, Iowa*

*I tell you the truth, you will weep…*
*while the world rejoices…*
*but your grief will turn to joy.*
*John 16:20*

# Let Me Show You My Pictures

## ▰▰ Joy Buster

**Be Joyful!**
**Who me? I forgot to bring the latest pictures of my grandchildren!**

## ▰▰ Joy Booster

How can a grandmother keep from smiling when she hears her grandchildren saying things that their mother said as a child? How can her heart keep from jumping for joy when she sees their hands folded while offering their simple prayers? When raising children, we have endless magnificent opportunities to praise God for his steadfastness in our lives! *Your life has a purpose,* including the opportunity to now mentor the younger generation about God's grace in *your* life. Whether you live close or far from your grandchildren, your godly influence can make a difference in future generations. Start with what you can do; don't stop because of what you can't do. Proclaim the difference between the world's false kind of happiness and God's everlasting joy! Be diligent telling them that you

125

love them. Remind them often of God's love and salvation. Life is full of golden opportunities. Flow with God's magnetic love! ***Grab Joy – and your pictures – and Go show them to someone!***

## Joy Injection

> *For we are God's workmanship,*
> *created in Christ Jesus to do good works,*
> *which God prepared in advance for us to do.*
> *Ephesians 2:10*

## Joy Connection

Gracious and most faithful Father,
I praise You for the real joy I find in...
Forgive me for...
Help me to make a difference today by...

# Inject a spirit of joy and optimism into your grandchildren. Do it by example!

# JOY Burst

## Be Joyful?
### Yes I can, even when…

Statistics show that there are a growing number of
grandparents raising grandchildren. My husband and I
are among them. It wasn't what we planned for our
retirement years, but God had other plans for us in His
mission field.

I was overwhelmed when we first took our four
grandchildren into our home. I said to a friend, "I only
had three children the first time, but now that I am
older, I have four." She replied, "God wants you to put
your hands to the plow and not look back."

When we first took the two and a half year old
twins into our home, one of them stood looking at a
poster I had hanging on a door. It was Jesus holding an
aborted baby, with a bag of aborted babies at His feet.
In her baby-talk voice she said, "That Jesus. He holding me." How did she know she was almost an
abortion?

How did she know Jesus? Her parents did have her
baptized but neglected to talk to her about Him. The
power of the Holy Spirit was truly at work. The joy
that filled my heart at that moment was only from the
Lord!

God promised to always be with me, and He was. I
trusted Him for guidance, wisdom and to give me a

sense of humor. I'll never forget the day the twins were bathing and said, "When you get old grandma, we will take care of you. We'll put you in the bathtub and give you a bath!" The laughter at that moment seemed to erase the pain from my two back surgeries.

In both the joys and the sorrows, I knew the joy of the Lord would always be my strength! Great is His faithfulness, even in changing circumstances!

Have faith in God's plans!
*Joy Burst Bea Daily, Florida*

*For great is his love toward us,
and the faithfulness of the Lord endures forever.
Psalm 117:2*

# Life Is a Journey Not a Destination

## ▰▰▰ Joy Buster

**Be Joyful!**
**Who me? I'm overwhelmed!**

## ▰▰▰ Joy Booster

A clock had been running for a long, long time on the mantel piece. One day the clock began to think about how many times during the year ahead it would have to tick. It counted up the seconds: 31,536,000 in one year. The old clock just got too tired and said, "I can't do it." It stopped right there. When somebody reminded the clock that it didn't have to tick the 31,536,000 seconds all at once but rather one-by-one, it began to run again and everything was all right.*

It's easy to feel overwhelmed! Without realizing it, others manage your time and plan your schedule. It takes maximum effort and realistic planning to function in today's instant, fast-paced world!

God doesn't ask you to win the title "Champion of Doing the Most." He just asks you to be faithful as the clock ticks away. Before you begin your day, fill up in His Word for guidance, top it off with prayer about your *to do list* and then follow as the Spirit leads. Let enthusiasm, *God in you*, be your password for the day! **Grab Joy and Go!**

*Taken from an old McGuffey Reader

## Joy Injection

> *Everything has its own time,*
> *and there is a specific time*
> *for every activity under heaven.*
> *Ecclesiastes 3:1 GW*

## Joy Connection

Wonderful Counselor,
I praise You for the real joy I find in...
Forgive me for...
Help me to make a difference today by...

# Feed your faith and watch your doubts starve to death.

# Looking Up

## Joy Buster

**Be Joyful!**
**Who me? How can I when I do what I don't**
**want to do, and don't do what I want to do?**

## Joy Booster

Once upon a time there was an elderly man who as he walked down the street, would occasionally stop and look up. Finally someone asked him, "Why do you stop and look up so much? It takes you so long to get anywhere." "Oh," he said, "Whenever I have a thought that is not pleasing to my Lord, I stop and confess it."*

Look up and confess your sins. Bask in the freedom of God's forgiveness. Then reach out and forgive others, just as you have been forgiven. No strings attached. Forgiveness brings true joy – to both the one who gives and the one who receives! ***Grab Joy and Go!***

*Story source unknown

## Joy Injection

*If we claim to be without sin,*
*we deceive ourselves and the truth is not in us.*
*If we confess our sins, he is faithful and just*
*and will forgive us our sins and purify us*
*from all unrighteousness.*
*1 John 1:8-9*

131

## Joy Connection

Jesus, my Savior,
I praise You for the real joy I find in...
Forgive me for...
Help me to make a difference today by...

## Forgiveness is giving love when there is no reason.

## JOY-Toon

Hurray for technology!
Reboot, reboot, reboot...
but with Joy!

# JOY Burst

## Be Joyful?
### Yes I can, even when...

"You are forgiven." It had taken more than 50 years to say those words. After receiving a telephone call that my mother was very ill with congestive heart failure, my husband and I traveled many hundreds of miles to visit my mother in a Yuma, Arizona, hospital.

As I sat in the room, I realized that there was an unresolved problem that needed to be addressed. With the strength of the Holy Spirit, I said to my mother, "I forgave you many years ago for leaving me with my grandparents. In fact, I want to thank you for doing so because my living with my grandparents gave me an opportunity to know Christ." I told her that I was sorry that I had not shared this with her so many years earlier.

Immediately, it was visible by my mother's body language and words that a great weight had been lifted from her body and soul. We embraced and prayed. I wanted to make sure that she still knew the Christ that she had known as a child.

*Hope*

God is so good. With His love and forgiveness, we are able to forgive others. Forgiveness produces peace and joy.

Always trust God for guidance!
*Joy Burst Ida Mall, Colorado*

*Be kind and compassionate to one another,
forgiving each other, just as
in Christ God forgave you.
Ephesians 4:32*

## JOY-Toon

A JOY-filled
Rx is looking at
life through
the eyes of
Christ!

# Marred But Useful

![joybuster] **Joy Buster**

**Be Joyful!**
**Who me? How can I, when I feel so**
**hopeless?**

![joybooster] **Joy Booster**

Imagine watching a potter at his wheel. His large
gorgeous creation is almost finished when suddenly,
he smashes it. Would you be shocked? "How can he
do that? It looked flawless." Your Potter looks beyond
and sees what marred vessels can become. David, who
committed adultery, wrote joy-laced scripture. Peter,
marred by his denial of Christ, was restored, and bold-
ly proclaimed God's love. Marred by her vocation,
Rahab, a prostitute, played a pivotal role in helping the
Israelites take the Promised
Land. She is listed in the
"Faith Hall of Fame"
(Hebrews 12:31). Jesus
*delights* in choosing the most
unlikely people to be His love
in action! Transformation
begins when you see
yourself through

135

Christ's eyes! Explode with praise! Burst with joy! He has chosen *you*! ***Grab Joy and Go and glow!***

## Joy Injection

*Being confident of this, that he who began*
*a good work in you will carry it on to completion*
*until the day of Christ Jesus.*
*Philippians 1:6*

## Joy Connection

Master Potter,
I praise You for the real joy I find in...
Forgive me for...
Help me to make a difference today by...

# God doesn't look at your past to determine your future.

# Marred and Magnificent, God Can Use You Too!

Abraham was too old.

Methuselah, way too old.

David, a shepherd, was too young.

Peter was afraid of death and impulsive.

John was self-righteous.

Naomi was a widow.

Jonah ran away from God.

Miriam was a gossip.

Moses stuttered.

Gideon and Thomas doubted.

Jeremiah was depressed and suicidal.

Elijah was burned out.

Martha was a worry wart.

Samson had long hair.

Noah was prone to unrealistic building projects and got drunk.

Moses and Paul had a short fuse.

Timothy had ulcers.

Amos's only training was in the school of fig-tree pruning.

Jacob was a liar.

Solomon was too rich.

Rahab was a harlot.

Adam had problems with his wife.

Deborah, a female, was a judge.

*You did not choose me, but I chose you and appointed you to go and bear fruit—fruit that will last.*
*John 15:16a*

# Marvelous Maneuvers

God's Word is filled with exercises. Invite your friends and neighbors over and workout together!

| | |
|---|---|
| Genesis 13:17 | "Arise,walk!" |
| | [Stand and walk in place ] |
| Psalm 47:1 | "Clap your hands all you people!" |
| | [Clap hands ] |
| Exodus 3:5 | "Put off your shoes from your feet." |
| | [Take off shoes ] |
| Psalm 139:2a | "You know when I sit …"[Sit down ] |
| Psalm 139:2b | "…and when I rise up."[Stand up ] |
| Luke 6:21 | "For you shall laugh."[Laugh ] |
| Jeremiah 8:14 | "Why do we sit still?"[Sit quietly ] |
| Proverbs 24:33 | "A little folding of the hands." |
| | [Say a silent prayer ] |
| Jeremiah 7:13 | "Rise up early."[Stand quickly ] |
| Ecclesiastes 3:5 | "A time to embrace …" |
| | [Hug each other ] |

Adapted from "Exercising To His Word," Karol Selle, The Lutheran Women's Missionary League, The Lutheran Church--Missouri Synod

# Me, a Bubbleologist?

### Joy Buster

**Who me? I don't know if I want to be a bubbleologist or not. Do I?**

### Joy Booster

According to the dictionary, to bubble means to display irrepressible activity or emotion. Combine that with a Christian's real source of joy and you are a bubbleologist! It is a liberating feeling to be a bubbleologist because your work is not limited to a day, time, year, or style. Each child of God expresses joy in her *own* unique way. You may erupt with so much enthusiasm that your feet can't be nailed to the floor. Or you might quietly bubble within. Whether you carry the joy of the Lord's presence like Martha or like Mary, when their brother Lazarus died, you can't keep your faith hidden even in the worst situations. People will *know* Jesus Christ is in your life because of the way you live life, show love, and tell of His love! Start a Joy Squad! Be contagious. Cause an epidemic. Invite everyone to be a bubbleologist! ***Grab Joy and Go bubble!***

## Joy Injection

> *Those who say that they live in him*
> *must live the same way he lived.*
> *1 John 2:6 GW*

## Joy Connection

Jesus, Source of Everlasting Joy,
I praise You for the real joy I find in...
Forgive me for...
Help me to make a difference today by...

**A person cannot communicate
to another any joy except
that of which she is herself conscious.**

# Mirror, Mirror on the Wall

## Joy Buster

**Be Joyful!**
**Who me? I wonder if I'm attractive?**

## Joy Booster

What do you see when you look in the mirror? Skin that's maturing, hair that looks drab, teeth that need whitening? Products are continually being improved to give you that flawless look. All the ads say that they will give you value. Not so! The authentic Beauty Manual, God's Word, tells you that *true* beauty comes from your *personal relationship* with the Lord. In God's eyes, you have both beauty and purpose.

Through this unique Christian perspective, you can build a truly fulfilling identity as a woman — an identity that will attract others to you and to your Lord. He will bring out the best in you, just as He did with Queen Esther.* In dedication to her Lord and His cause, Queen Esther selflessly used her beauty for the benefit

141

of her people. Jesus accepts you wholeheartedly, so why don't you? When you look in the mirror, look for Christ's reflection. Be contagious with His real beauty and glow from His indwelling! *Grab Joy and Go!*

* Esther 1-10

## Joy Injection

*Don't become so well-adjusted to your culture*
*that you fit into it without even thinking.*
*Instead, fix your attention on God.*
*You'll be changed from the inside out.*
*Readily recognize what he wants from you,*
*and quickly respond to it. Unlike the culture*
*around you, always dragging you down to its level*
*of immaturity, God brings the best out of you,*
*develops well-formed maturity in you.*
*Romans 12:2 MSG*

## Joy Connection

Powerful Creator,
I praise You for the real joy I find in...
Forgive me for...
Help me to make a difference today by...

# When you arrive in heaven no one will ask you how much you weigh! You'll be perfect!

# New and Improved? Never!

## ◼ Joy Buster

**Be Joyful!**
**Who me? How can I when one day**
**something is supposed to be permanent and**
**the next day it isn't?**

## ◼ Joy Booster

Women tend to experiment with various brands until
they find one they like and then they keep buying it.
They use it for years until suddenly it becomes *new
and improved* or even worse, discontinued. Nothing is
permanent except Jesus Christ! Beware, though,
because Satan is ecstatic when his joy robbers infiltrate
your heart and mind. He draws your attention to all
your bills, then you forget to give thanks for the
ones you have paid. He
discourages you with the
cost of medications
when you can
be thankful
there are
drugs to give
relief. Lucifer
consumes you
with the big
picture concerns,

God's JOY is
permanent!

143

so you will take for granted the mini blessings which bring opportunities for joy! In a changing world you can trust your unchanging God! Shout it from the mountaintop — *God's joy is permanent!* ***Grab Joy and Go!***

## Joy Injection

*Jesus Christ is the same yesterday, today, and forever.*
*Hebrews 13:8 GW*

## Joy Connection

Dear Constant Source of my joy,
I praise You for the real joy I find in...
Forgive me for...
Help me to make a difference today by...

# We cannot become what we need to be by remaining what we are.

Max DePree

# JOY Burst

## Be Joyful?
### Yes I can, even when...

Being a practical, methodical, retired couple we
weren't even looking for a house until a Sunday drive
to a small town changed our minds.

The large English-style stone house just seemed to
beckon to us, and it was for sale! Within ten days our
"wonder what it looks like inside" was a "congratula-
tions on your new home!" We were stunned, but it was
perfect...except that the window panes all needed
replacing and a hall carpet was in bad shape.

A month later we were in and settled...until the
painter stepped through a window sill and we found
that the original window casings were bad and every
window had to be completely replaced. Then the roots
of a large tree caused foundation problems...and
cracked the tile flooring, which had to be removed
and replaced by wooden floors. It was beginning to
resemble the Tom Hank's movie, <u>The</u> <u>Money</u> <u>Pit</u>!

Somehow, the Lord led us to remember that movie
and encouraged us to laugh. We grumbled at first, but
as one problem after another appeared, it became
apparent that it was better to laugh than to cry or get
angry. We found that following the directive of

Ephesians 4:31(Authorized KJV) to *let all bitterness and anger be put away from you,* resulted in the truth of Proverbs 15:13; *a happy heart makes a cheerful face.* Would we buy the house again? Yes, but we'd probably offer less!

Rejoice in all things!
*Joy Burst Dolores Bruncke,*
*Texas*

*In every thing give thanks....*
*1 Thessalonians 5:18 KJV*

# New Challenges

## Joy Buster

**Be Joyful!**
**Who me? That's not as easy as it sounds!**
**I've never done it that way before. I'm**
**scared of the unknown.**

## Joy Booster

God did not give Moses a sneak preview of the parting
of the Red Sea so he would be confident that the
unknown would be safe to do. Moses had to *trust*
and go. Like Moses, walk in faith to your Red Sea
challenge! God's timing, even through unique
challenges, is *perfect* for you! The joy of the
Lord will be your
strength – always.
***Grab Joy and***
***Go in faith!***

## Joy Injection

*Have I not commanded you?*
*Be strong and courageous. Do not be terrified;*
*do not be discouraged, for the Lord your God*
*will be with you wherever you go.*
*Joshua 1:9*

## Joy Connection

Dear Heavenly Father,
I praise You for the real joy I find in...
Forgive me for...
Help me to make a difference today by...

**The person who knows
where she stands with God
can feel joy in any situation
for real joy is not dependent
on externals
but His internal presence.**

148

# Nothing Is Happening!

## ▬ Joy Buster

**Be Joyful!**
**Who me? No matter how hard I work, it**
**looks like nothing is happening!**

## ▬ Joy Booster

A modern-day parable says that once upon a time the
Lord appeared to a woman. He explained that He had
work for her to do. Every day she was to push, with
all her strength, against a massive rock in her yard.
After years of pushing against the rock without ever
moving it, she felt all her work was in vain. Sensing
her discouragement, Satan decided to enter the picture.
"Nothing is happening," he taunted. "Give up; it's
hopeless!" The woman intended to quit but to first

make it a matter of prayer. "Lord, I've pushed with all my strength, but the rock has not moved." The Lord replied, "My child, you have done just as I asked. I never once mentioned that I expected you to move the rock. Look at your arms, legs and hands. They are much stronger now. Through opposition, you have grown. Your calling was to be obedient and to put your faith and trust in My wisdom. This you have done. Now, my beloved, I will help you move the rock!"*

Jesus, the Rock of your salvation, asks you to press forward in your daily walk, totally trusting Him. It is difficult to be patient and obedient when you can't see anything happening. But helplessness does not mean hopelessness. You may not see God's big picture for your life, but you can learn to put your faith in action! Faith means looking at what Christ has done in the past, yielding every breath you take to Him in the future and not listening to Satan's discouraging words! Read God's Word daily. Meditate on it. Apply it. This injection of joy will go straight to your downcast spirit and revitalize your disposition. Then with confidence, not fear, you can move through life's changing circumstances. *Grab Joy and Go push!*

*Story Source Unknown

## ■ Joy Injection

*Trust in the Lord with all your heart and*
*lean not on your own understanding;*
*in all your ways acknowledge him,*
*and he will make your paths straight.*
*Proverbs 3:5-6*

## ■ Joy Connection

Father, You are my Rock,
I praise You for the real joy I find in...
Forgive me for...
Help me to make a difference today by...

# The will of God will never take you where the face of God will not protect you.

# OK, Joy Is My Choice. What's Yours?

### ▨ Joy Buster

**Be Joyful!**
**Who me? I can't decide which one to choose.**

### ▨ Joy Booster

The circumstances were rotten and the prospects were grim! Paul and Silas were falsely accused, beaten by a hostile crowd and tossed into prison; yet they chose to sing and worship God. How could they find joy at a time like this? They trusted God's promise to always be with them and that something good would come out of this devastation.*

152

Choosing God's joy, which is always available, will make an amazing difference in your daily walk. His joy is never linked to circumstances but to a consistent relationship with Jesus Christ. Be energized from God's Word! Trust Your Shepherd's love to encompass you in your daily routine. When you choose joy you are deciding to walk by faith, not by sight. The joy of the Lord is your strength—always! Choose joy! *Grab Joy and Go!*

*Acts 16

## Joy Injection

*Be joyful always; pray continually;*
*give thanks in all circumstances,*
*for this is God's will for you in Christ Jesus.*
*1 Thessalonians 5:16-18*

## Joy Connection

Loving Shepherd...
I praise you for the real joy I find in...
Forgive me for...
Help me to make a difference today by...

# Joy multiplies
# when you spread it around!

# JOY Burst

## Be Joyful?
### Yes I can, even when...

It was during the bleakest hour of my life that I experienced a "living truth." I had just been confronted with the traumatic realization that my marriage, already riddled with the effects of alcoholism, had a new layer of betrayal, deceit, and humiliation.

The pain was more overwhelming than I had ever imagined possible. Nothing – not thoughts of my three precious children, not the foundation of a life-long faith in a loving Creator – nothing seemed able to alleviate that intense pain. I wanted out of my office, my surroundings, my life.

I borrowed a co-worker's car with the intent of driving to one of the winding, mountain roads that encircled our small town and pulling in front of a logging truck. "The relentless agony would end," I thought.

I was on the highway. I could hear a logging truck approaching, so I steeled my grip on the steering wheel. And then, the Lord of life and joy did the most incredible thing. God placed in my mind this thought, "When my co-worker finds out I wrecked his car, he is going to kill me." Strange? Bizarre? Not really. You see, the God who had created me with my skewed sense of humor knew that He could use it to get my attention.

The "living truth" was that our Lord not only counts the hairs on our head, but He even takes the

155

time to speak in our "language." God loved me enough to make me laugh at that critical time, and my laughter sparked a tiny bit of hope, a hope that said my worth was purchased on a cross, not based on the human validation, a hope that said I had choices, a hope that said only my Savior could bring strength, healing and joy back into my shattered life. And He most certainly did. He is there for you too!

God works in mysterious ways!
*Joy Burst Jan Struck,*
*Wisconsin*

*No temptation has seized you except what is
common to man. And God is faithful; he will not let
you be tempted beyond what you can bear.
But when you are tempted, he will also provide
a way out so that you can stand up under it.*
*1 Corinthians 10:13*

# Only If, Then I Would Be Happy

![Joy Buster] **Joy Buster**

**Be Joyful!**
**Who me? I have so many wants! If only I**
**could feel really happy!**

![Joy Booster] **Joy Booster**

"If only I could shop at Wal-Mart and buy everything I want, then I'd be happy." "If only I could be in the bathroom without someone knocking on the door, then I'd be happy!" "If only I could have a bigger house, a new car...then I would be happy!" So often we look for happiness in all the wrong places. God's Word says that a thankful heart is a happy heart. To have complete happiness, you must enter into the Lord's presence with thanksgiving. When you appreciate all that you already have, especially His love, you'll see your circumstances and possessions in proper perspective, and happiness *will not* elude you. As you grow in your

157

personal relationship with Jesus Christ, your focus will shift from activities and things that make you momentarily happy to faith's lasting values that erupt in permanent hallelujahs! ***Grab Joy and Go!***

## Joy Injection

*Enter with the password: "Thank you!"*
*Make yourselves at home, talking praise.*
*Thank him. Worship him.*
*Psalm 100:4 MSG*

## Joy Connection

My Restorer,
I praise You for the real joy I find in...
Forgive me for...
Help me to make a difference today by...

# Joy is not in things, it is in us.

Benjamin Franklin

# Original or Copy?

### ▰▰ Joy Buster

**Be Joyful!**
**Who me? If I'm an original, then why do I**
**want to be like everybody else?**

### ▰▰ Joy Booster

People are born originals, but most of them will die a
copy. Peer pressure, trends and fads seem to magnetize
people because they don't want to stand out as
*different*. As you grow in your relationship with Jesus
Christ, you will become more confident that you are
exactly the way He planned you. To copy others is to
cheat yourself out of the fullness of what God has
called you to be and to do. Rejoice in that fact, and
you will feel contentment! Submit to the Lord and
you can be the best original joy-filled you that God
intended you to be! ***Grab Joy and Go!***

### ▰▰ Joy Injection

*I praise you because I am fearfully*
*and wonderfully made;*
*your works are wonderful, I know that full well.*
*Psalm 139:14*

## Joy Connection

Dear Creator of Originality,
I praise You for the real joy I find in...
Forgive me for...
Help me to make a difference today by...

**Satan's mission is accomplished when you focus on the negative instead of the positive.**

## JOY-Toon

Ener-JOY-zing
always starts with
a good charge!

# Plans for Today

## Joy Buster

**Be Joyful!**
**Who me? I felt overwhelmed. How could I**
**get everything done? I made the**
**perfect to-do list, and then nothing went**
**according to my plan. Stress!**

## Joy Booster

When circumstances do not happen according to your plan, remember Who is really in charge of your day. God knows all the events of your life, including even the tiny, insignificant details. Anticipate change and *accept* interruptions as God's good plans specifically designed for you! After all, this is the day the Lord has made. There is always reason to rejoice! His joy is ever-present even when life's circumstances don't make you happy. *Grab Joy and Go enjoy how God planned your day!*

## Joy Injection

*For I know the plans I have for you, declares the Lord,*
*plans to prosper you and not to harm you,*
*plans to give you hope and a future.*
*Jeremiah 29:11*

## Joy Connection

Dear Heavenly Father,
I praise You for the real joy I find in...
Forgive me for...
Help me to make a difference today by...

**When you look back on your life,
you'll regret the things you didn't do
more than the things you did.**

# JOY Burst

## Be Joyful?
### Yes I can, even when...

September 11, 2001, was a typical workday in the
Pentagon. That morning we held a joyous birthday
party for a co-worker. As we returned to our own work
area, we received word about the attacks on the World
Trade Center. It seemed only a few minutes later when
the Pentagon shook violently, setting off screaming fire
alarms and flashing strobe lights. I knew immediately
that we were under attack.

I headed for the door into the hallway. Smoke was
beginning to fill the hall as people exited their offices.
Some people ran out of fear, while others calmly
walked out of the building. Unlike many people that
day, I survived.

Since the 9/11 attack, I have spent many hours in
prayer, read inspirational books and attended a
women's Christian retreat. Each of these events opened
my eyes to several important truths. First, I have
learned that good things can come from the terrible
actions of evil people.

That day in September caused me to step back a
moment, to reassess my beliefs, to allow God to
strengthen my faith through His Word, and to count
my many blessings. I have also learned again that the
Lord is always standing beside me just as He was there

when I learned I had cancer. Jesus said, *I am with you always, even to the end of the age* (Matthew 28:20).

God was there as I ran from the Pentagon. I will fear no evil. I will be brave when my mind takes me back to September 11 because *God is [my] refuge and strength, a very present help in trouble* (Psalm 46:1). His grace is sufficient for all my needs and by His grace Jesus Christ lives in my heart each day.

Trust in Him – totally!
*Joy Burst Nancy Barth,*
*Virginia*

*I will praise you forever for what you have done;*
*in your name I will hope, for your name is good.*
*I will praise you in the presence of your saints.*
*Psalm 52:9*

# Puzzled and Frustrated!

## Joy Buster

**Be Joyful!**
**Who me? I can't seem to do anything right.**

## Joy Booster

A woman once gave two puzzles to a friend for a gift.
As a joke she switched the box tops. The friend, who
used the box top as a guide, soon became frustrated
because the pieces and the picture didn't match. She
tried the second puzzle with the same results. The
gift-giver confessed the prank, and then everything fit
together according to the picture.*

We experience similar frustrations in understanding our identity when we look at the picture offered to
us by the world.

There, identity hinges on external things such as how we look, with whom we socialize, what we own, even our career. Satan leads us to believe that there will be someone at the heavenly gate asking, "What's your financial status? What size

165

dress do you wear? Do you have any gray hairs?"
How quickly we can lose sight that our world-pro-
nounced identity has nothing to do with our salvation.
There is no puzzle to your identity when it's grounded
in Jesus Christ! See yourself through His eyes:
unconditionally loved, totally forgiven, and gifted
with eternal life! Being grounded in His grace is a
liberating force in how we interact with others and
how we walk life's mountains and valleys. Keep your
joy-light on! ***Grab Joy and Go!***

*Story Source Unknown

## Joy Injection

> *Don't be afraid, I've redeemed you.*
> *I've called your name. You're mine.*
> *Isaiah 43:1b MSG*

## Joy Connection

Jesus, I belong to You,
I praise You for the real joy I find in...
Forgive me for...
Help me to make a difference today by...

## Caution: As a child of God, you'll experience the most incredible joy imaginable!

# JOY Burst

## Be Joyful?
### Yes I can, even when...

There I was in the middle of our LWML meeting. The year was 1988. I was listening to a speaker from the Crisis Pregnancy Center talking about her past abortion. No one in the room knew about my abortion 15 years earlier, not even my 13 year-old daughter sitting next to me.

When the speaker talked about forgiveness for her abortion, I thought, "How could this be?" I tried to forget about my abortion, but because I continued to have a great deal of sadness and guilt, I could not stop having all those "bad" feelings. I thought that I wasn't forgiven at all!

Over 3,000 women have abortions each day, but this speaker was the only person I met who had talked openly about having had an abortion. After the meeting I met with her and realized a lot of things about forgiveness. You see, I never admitted that I had sinned when I paid money to abort my baby.

*When I kept silent, my bones grew old through my groaning all the day long...I acknowledged my sin to You, and my iniquity I have not hidden...And You forgave the iniquity of my sin* (Psalm 32:3-5). These verses described the last 15 years of my life, how my "secret" sin caused both my spirit and my physical body to be tortured day and night.

When I confessed that my abortion was a sin, I was able to understand what Jesus had purchased for me on the cross. *He wanted me to have life more abundant. He heals the brokenhearted and binds up their wounds* (Psalms 147:3). Jesus had made my life full of hope and joy.

I told my daughter about my abortion, and now I tell whoever will listen because I know that other women need the joy that Jesus gives.

God's forgiveness always frees us!
*Joy Burst Jo Ann Epperson, Texas*

*Blessed be the God and Father*
*of our Lord Jesus Christ,*
*The Father of mercies and God of all comfort,*
*who comforts us in all our tribulation,*
*that we may be able to comfort*
*those who are in any trouble, by the comfort*
*with which we ourselves are comforted by God.*
*2 Corinthians 1:3-4 KJV*

# Rejoice or Be Happy

## Joy Buster

**Be Joyful!**
**Who me? Not me. I'm not rejoicing today,**
**or am I?**

## Joy Booster

How can St. Paul tell you to rejoice always? Did he
ever get in traffic jams, buy cereal to feed a family, or
listen to the whining at the church voters' meetings?
Does he know what it's like to measure up to the
bionic woman and run three kids in three different
directions at the same time? Has
he ever talked to the woman
raising her grandchild or to a
lonely widow? People,
including Christians, confuse
the meaning of happiness and
rejoicing. Happiness is centered
on something within yourself.
Rejoicing is *in* the Lord. "*We
are troubled on every side* (How
can anything else go wrong?),
yet not distressed. *We are
perplexed* (Why me?) *but not in
despair, persecuted but not
forsaken, cast down but not*

169

*destroyed*" (2 Corinthians 4:8-9). You can always count your blessings! God gives a joy which consequences cannot quench. His is a peace that circumstances cannot steal. Rejoice in the freedom to rejoice! ***Grab Joy and Go!***

## Joy Injection

> *Always be joyful in the Lord!*
> *I'll say it again: Be joyful!*
> *Philippians 4:4 GW*

## Joy Connection

Heavenly Advocate,
I praise You for the real joy I find in...
Forgive me for...
Help me to make a difference today by...

**Joy is happiness, but it is more:**
**It is a spiritual awareness**
**that something has entered you**
**and you know that you will never**
**be the same again.**

# Relax, Tell It Like It Is

## ▬▬ Joy Buster

**Be Joyful!
Who me? I want to squirm every time I have
to give witness of my faith.**

## ▬▬ Joy Booster

Remain calm. After all you are filled with God's
presence. In His presence there is joy. His joy gives
you strength. Moved by His Spirit, you can tell in your
own unique way how Jesus Christ has been your
refuge and your strength. Share how you strive to keep
going on because of your personal relationship with
Him. Include the joy you have in eternal life too. Refer
to God's Word. You'll be amazed how it will bless
your message. He simply asks you to *go and make
disciples,* not force them to convert to *your* opinions.
Focus on Him and you can do it! ***Grab Joy and Go!***

## Joy Injection

*Have I not commanded you?*
*Be strong and courageous.*
*Do not be terrified; do not be discouraged,*
*for the Lord your God*
*will be with you wherever you go.*
*Joshua 1:9*

## Joy Connection

Heavenly Father, calmer of my nerves,
I praise You for the real joy I find in...
Forgive me for...
Help me to make a difference today by...

**The difference between**
**catching men and catching fish**
**is that you catch fish**
**that are alive, and they die,**
**and you catch men that are dead**
**and bring them to life again.**

Robert D. Foster

# Be Joyful?
## Yes I can, even when...

From the early morning when her feet hit the ground until late at night, my four-foot seven-inch mother had always run circles around everyone else. Then she slowly slipped into another world where the darkness of Alzheimer's and Parkinson's disease zapped her of her energy for life.

When my son got married, I went to my parents' room in the hotel to help Mother get dressed. I asked her if she had slept well and she replied, "Yes, and I slept with a man last night." She continued, "But he has been dead for years." I looked at my dad and asked him how he felt about that. He responded he wasn't even aware he was sick, much less dead. We laughed so hard we were crying. While mother had no idea what was so funny, my dad and I became aware at that moment of God's gift to us of laughter. It would help us during those trying times.

Mother continued to slip into another world while my father and I looked for humor in the midst of many situations where laughter might not have seemed to be appropriate. The memories we share of those difficult days are sprinkled with the assurance we received whenever He seemed to whisper, "Lighten up." So now I encourage others to laugh, 'til you have tears in your eyes; you'll know in your heart it is a gift from the One who loves you most.

Mother got to the point that we couldn't understand what she was saying. One evening as they sat together, mother looked over to my dad, and with a twinkle in her eye, clearly stated, "I love you." My dad's heart was filled with such joy at that moment. The next morning my dear dad awoke to find the Lord had restored His lovely "child" named Mary, as He rewarded her with her heavenly crown. What a gift God gave to my father with those three simple words, "I love you," from my mother's lips before she slipped away for the last time.

God does provide joy bursts in spite of shadows!
*Joy Burst Edie Norris, Washington*

*I am greatly encouraged; in all our troubles my joy knows no bounds.*
*2 Corinthians 7:4*

# Resurrection Power!

## ▰▰▰ Joy Buster

**Be Joyful!**
**Who me? How can I? I just buried my**
**loved one.**

## ▰▰▰ Joy Booster

People are occasionally accused of not listening when others speak. Be assured that Jesus hears you even when you whisper, "What do I do now?" or "How do I muddle through this legal stuff?" Not one of your sighs is hidden from His heart. You have His full attention! He cuddles you in His arms as you mourn. His ceaseless love wipes each teardrop from broken dreams and plans. Jesus' love encompasses your life here on earth and in Heaven. Feeling vulnerable now does not mean life is hopeless. Your hope is in His resurrection! Even during bereavement, there is joy in His presence. ***Grab Joy and Go in faith!***

## ▰▰▰ Joy Injection

*"And surely I am with you always,*
*to the very end of the age.*
*Matthew 28:20b*

175

## Joy Connection

Jesus, my Savior,
I praise You for the real joy I find in...
Forgive me for...
Help me to make a difference today by...

**When faithfulness is most difficult,
it is most necessary
because trying times
are no time to quit trying.**

## JOY-Toon

# JOY Burst

## Be Joyful?
### Yes I can, even when...

After nearly 52 years of a great marriage I found myself alone. My husband had a lengthy illness; yet I was not prepared for the empty spot that his death left in my heart.

It would have been easy to lock all the doors and not go out. The drive to church was difficult, but the walk from the car and through the church doors was even more difficult. Our church family was wonderful and supportive; it was just so difficult doing it alone without my friend and companion of all those years.

I had not been active in church while care-giving and I didn't know what God wanted me to do with my life now. My prayer group helped me pray for God's direction. God was faithful to His promises. He did indeed have a purpose for me to fulfill. The chorus of the song, "Because He Lives" still brings tears to my eyes: "Because He lives, I can face tomorrow;…all fear is gone,…He holds the future. And life is worth living just because He lives." Knowing that I was always in Christ's presence and never alone, not even on those very empty nights, has given me strength and comfort!

My encouragement to others would be to not shut the doors, but make the difficult choice to move on and keep busy. Choose activities that are useful and productive, something that gives you great joy in doing. Remember to give yourself time to heal spiritually, emotionally and physically. God's Word is laced with hope. It was a magnificent source of hope and joy for me. May it strengthen you too.

My JOY was in God's presence!
*Joy Burst Jacquie Ingalls,*
*Oregon*


*And we pray this in order that you may*
*live a life worthy of the Lord*
*and may please him in every way;*
*bearing fruit in every good work,*
*growing in the knowledge of God,*
*being strengthened with all power*
*according to his glorious might*
*so that you may have great endurance and patience*
*and joyfully giving thanks to the Father,*
*who has qualified you to share in the inheritance*
*of the saints in the kingdom of light.*
*Colossians 1:10-12*

# Serve Fruit Daily

## Joy Buster

**Be Joyful!**
**Who me? I can't find joy!**

## Joy Booster

The answer to finding permanent joy is immersing
oneself in a personal relationship with Jesus Christ!
Start saturating yourself with what God has to say
about Himself and the joy He desires for you. Spend
time in His Word, in prayer, and obey His commands.
Live each moment in submission to God. Seek to
please Him as you share the gracious habits that only
the Holy Spirit can produce in you...love, joy, peace,
patience, kindness, goodness, faithfulness, gentleness
and self-control (Galatians 5:22-23). You will find
genuine joy *only* in the things of God. His joy
weathers the shocks of life because God is always
there! Fix your *focus on Jesus*, not your

179

gloomy circumstance — on the eternal, not the temporal. Joy is a sure sign of the presence of God in your life, a well-being that abides in your heart, knowing that all is well between yourself and the Lord. Jesus is your life-Source and your joy-giver. ***Grab Joy and Go share this Good News.***

## Joy Injection

*You did not choose me, but I chose you*
*and appointed you to go and bear fruit—*
*fruit that will last.*
*John 15:16a*

## Joy Connection

Source of all sources,
I praise You for the real joy I find in...
Forgive me for...
Help me to make a difference today by...

**It is not so much the joy of the Lord
we are seeking,
as the Lord of joy himself.**

C.S. Lewis

# Silent But Not Idle

Joy Buster

**Be Joyful!**
**Who me? Life is hopeless. God must have abandoned me!**

Joy Booster

A woman once said it was particularly painful to wake up in the morning feeling blue because she knew that depression had spent the night with her. Then she remembered the verse: *So these three things remain: faith, hope, and love. But the best one of these is love* (1 Corinthians 13:13 GW). She realized her hopeless feelings were crowding out her faith and God's love. (We often learn lessons in the darkness that we will never learn when all about us seems bright and peaceful.) Abraham believed in God when there was no human reason for hope. God may be silent but He is never idle. We may crowd Him out but He never deserts us! Open the door of your heart so He can join you as you...*Grab Joy and Go!*

Joy Injection

*I once was young, now I'm a graybeard—*
*not once have I seen an abandoned believer....*
*Psalm 37:25a MSG*

## Joy Connection

God of all hope,
I praise You for the real joy I find in...
Forgive me for...
Help me to make a difference today by...

## The devil is willing
## for you to confess your faith
## as long as you don't practice it.

## JOY-Toon

The owner only offers
free take outs....

...For us
to give
away!

# JOY Burst

## Be Joyful?
### Yes I can, even when...

Eighteen months after my husband died from his
lengthy cancer illness, my only living child died from
cancer. Eighteen months after that, I was hospitalized
with Cardiomyopathy. Eleven months later I had
surgery for potential cancer. While I was still hospitalized, I had a stroke. "Is this the way it is going to be
from now on? What are you trying to teach me God?"

I have survived only by the grace of God. I've
been strengthened by the joy of His everlasting
presence and trust, without one doubt, that nothing
will ever separate me from God's love. The Lord's
consolation brings joy to my soul. That thought is a
running dialogue between God and me, especially
when Satan fills me with anxiety and loneliness. The
resurrection gives me hope beyond this pilgrimage!

Morning is my favorite time of day! I feel the
warmth of the sun and His SON because His mercies
are new every morning! There is great comfort in
knowing that once again I can exchange all my
weakness for His powerful strength. He deletes my
mourning and inserts His unfailing love. There is an
awesome sense of security knowing this.

I have also been uplifted by others. People have no
idea how this medicates the hurting heart and implants
healing. Never take for granted the smallest acts of
kindness, such as sending cards after everyone else

forgets to, being a listener and not a gossip, staying for a visit when food is delivered, helping even when we deny the need — these are all joy boosters! Be obedient to the Holy Spirit, and you will know exactly what to say and do. *God has poured out His love into our hearts by the Holy Spirit* (Romans 5:5).

I challenge you to rejoice in all things because God's love is unfailing! Face each new day knowing that life is a journey and not a destination. This is what God is teaching me!

His love is everlasting!
*Joy Burst Ida Luebke,*
*Ohio*

*The Lord is my strength and my shield;*
*my heart trusts in him, and I am helped.*
*My heart leaps for joy*
*and I will give thanks to him in song.*
*Psalm 28:7*

# Take Joy Out of Hiding

## Joy Buster

**Be Joyful!**
**Who me? I'm bored when I travel if there**
**are no billboards to read. I like to know**
**what to expect.**

## Joy Booster

Billboards help travelers anticipate what's ahead. As
God's child, you are a billboard for Him. Wherever
you go, whatever you do, others will know what Christ
is like by your values, your conduct, your words and
lifestyle. That's a powerful thought, isn't it? Without
realizing it you can be God's best, or worst, billboard.
Enjoy your job as His public relations agent. "Your joy
is the joy of God passing through
you!"* Take joy out of hiding!
Begin an epidemic.
Spread joy! *Grab*
*Joy and*
*Go!*

*John MacArthur, Jr,
Liberty in Christ,
Word of Grace Communications,
Panorama City, CA

185

## Joy Injection

*The Lord has done spectacular things for us.*
*We are overjoyed.*
*Psalm 126:3 GW*

## Joy Connection

I come to You, O Redeemer,
I praise You for the real joy I find in...
Forgive me for...
Help me to make a difference today by...

# It is easier to preach ten sermons than to live one.

# Tell My Age?

## ▰▰ Joy Buster

**Be Joyful!**
**Who me? When I've just been surprised**
**with another over-the-hill party?**

## ▰▰ Joy Booster

Children can't wait to tell you their age – whether
they're 3 or 16. But, how do you react when people
ask you your age? Do you refuse to answer – or sub-
tract a few years? If you're a senior citizen, do you add
ten years so you will hear, "You look good for your
age!" Even if you don't like the new aches and pains,
the stronger eye glass prescription or smile lines that
grow deeper, each year offers new blessings. With
each birthday the Lord sends new opportunities to let
His light shine through you.
Change your attitude from
sadness to gladness by *focusing*
*on the way you age, not the*
*age you are*. Through
Christ, we can learn and
share His love no matter
how old we are. Go
ahead — let the world
have fun selling over-the-
hill decorations. Laugh

187

and enjoy all the teasing that comes with another birthday because you have real joy in the light of God's presence, not how many — or how few — candles are on your cake! ***Grab Joy and Go!***

## Joy Injection

*Even when you're old, I'll take care of you.*
*Even when your hair turns gray,*
*I'll support you.*
*I made you and will continue to care for you.*
*I'll support you and save you.*
*Isaiah 46:4 GW*

## Joy Connection

Dearest Father who created me,
I praise You for the real joy I find in...
Forgive me for...
Help me to make a difference today by...

**You are over the hill when in the morning you snap, crackle and pop, but it isn't breakfast cereal.**

# The 2:00 A.M. Phone Call

## Joy Buster

**Be Joyful!**
**Who me? I know when the phone rings in**
**the middle of the night, it's not good news.**

## Joy Booster

When we have aging parents, we can expect the phone
to ring when we least expect it. Caring for elderly
parents is often a revolving guilt trip. When we are
with them, we feel guilty because we are needed at
home. When we are at home, we feel guilty because
we are not with our parents. We wonder if we are making the right decision. We feel like everywhere we
turn, a Goliath overwhelms us. It's okay; cry and cry
some more. Tell God exactly how you feel; He will
listen! Draw guidance
from His Word in
order to deal

with each new challenge. *The more you fill your mind with the presence of the Lord*, the more His Light will shine and guide you into the unknown of reversing roles. Sling your trust in the Lord every time you encounter a Goliath! It wasn't the rock that killed the giant but David's faith! ***Grab Joy and Go — you will make it one day at a time!***

## Joy Injection

*Those who know your name will trust in you,*
*for you, Lord, have never forsaken those who seek you.*
*Psalm 9:10*

## Joy Connection

Heavenly Father and my Guidance Counselor,
I praise You for the real joy I find in...
Forgive me for...
Help me to make a difference today by...

## The task ahead is never as great as the Power behind us.

# JOY Burst

## Be Joyful?
### Yes I can, even when...

Seeing God work in the events that preceded my mother's death was quite an experience! Things were happening so rapidly that I hardly had time to think what to do next. I just felt numb, but I could see God's guidance so I kept *moving*.

Mother had always been a very intelligent, sharp woman, physically able to do most things. Just after my stepfather was admitted to a home for Alzheimer's patients, Mother *moved* to an assisted living facility. She was there because she was unable to care for herself. After just one week, the administrator informed me that Mother was dying. The director not only encouraged me to seek the help of hospice, but she made all the contacts. Once again, God provided for Mother's needs exactly when she needed them. She *moved* to the Hospice House for six days of medical monitoring. Now, for the next *move*!

Precisely the day we needed a nursing home to *move* Mother to, God opened a place for her at a facility close to my home. By the time she was settled there, she had experienced four different living arrangements in less than a month. She had every right to be confused; her whole world had changed drastically. One time she asked, "Is this the place I will stay?" I told her it was until Jesus came to take her to her real home, and that would be a heavenly *move!*

During her last days I spent time singing songs and reciting memorized scripture to her. It was then when I realized how dedicated she had been to living out her confirmation verse, *but one thing is necessary. Mary has chosen the good portion which will not be taken away from her* (Luke 10:42 ESV). I thought of how my mother had chosen the "good portion" the "one thing necessary." She had valued her time in the Word and spent time memorizing scripture and hymns. She insisted that I do it too. It was almost as if God were comforting me and saying that even while she lay dying, this was not taken away from her. What we had hidden in our hearts was now a fountain of Living Water, gushing forth with joy!

I encourage you to read God's word daily. Memorize it. Don't put it off. You never know when you will be on the MOVE and need His instant guiding Word!

Follow the nudge of the Holy Spirit!
*Joy Burst Jan Wendorf, Wisconsin*

*Let the word of Christ dwell in you richly*
*as you teach and admonish one another....*
*Colossians 3:16*

# The Joy Of Forgiving

## Joy Buster

**Be Joyful!**
**Who me? After what you did to me, why should I give you a second chance?**

## Joy Booster

Has your spouse, child, friend, family member or co-worker ever asked you for a second chance? Forgiveness is something each person deals with differently. What takes one person a short time to work through might be a long process for another. Sometimes we play the waiting game, expecting the other person to make restitution: if he apologizes, if she comes back to me, if he rehires me, if they clean up their room, if they never do that again…. Meanwhile we allow an unforgiving spirit to weave its way into the fabric of our lives. What a blessing that when it comes to the grace of God, *no* performance is required, no if's are involved. Our Lord asks only that we be sorry for the wrongs we commit.

193

Peter the disciple must have known that it's not every day people get a second chance, much less find someone who will give them a second chance every time they goof! Let the joy of God's forgiveness pump your adrenaline. Let it lead you to offer that second chance. Tell everyone about His awesome forgiveness! *Grab Joy and Go practice Christ's example.*

## Joy Injection

*Be kind and compassionate to one another,*
*forgiving each other,*
*just as in Christ God forgave you.*
*Ephesians 4:32*

## Joy Connection

Jesus, my Savior,
I praise You for the real joy I find in...
Forgive me for...
Help me to make a difference today by...

# God forgets the past; imitate Him.

Max Lucado

## Be Joyful?
### Yes I can, even when...

My drinking started very innocently in the fall of my high school junior year. A group of friends were at the bowling alley when a very handsome young man showed up in his little sports car. I liked to laugh and have a good time, so we piled in his car and he offered us a *Little King*. It didn't take much for me to feel a *buzz*. Now I really knew what "feeling good" was like and that was just the beginning.

I remained a good student at school, and my teachers respected me. Little did they know that I lived for the weekends when my friends and I could *party hardy* with alcohol. Many times I woke up only to run to the bathroom and hug the toilet. I often wondered how I got home, but the scary part was learning that I had driven my friends home.

Even though I looked forward to entering college, I didn't have anyone to prepare me for what was about to happen. My first roommate was a pot smoking, sexually active young woman and rich too! Coming from a good family in a small town, I was in culture shock. My worst fear of a roommate was coming true. I reminded myself that alcohol was much more acceptable than drugs (because my friends were doing that), but marijuana was a no-no. I didn't want my clothes smelling like pot, so I made up excuses to go home every weekend. My sole purpose was to be home and party with people who understood me.

Being home so frequently, I ran into a guy from high school who also liked to have a good time. After partying one night I ended up at his place. He put the "Queen of Hearts" card on the outside of his suite door. Little did I know what that meant...until it happened. The next morning I felt so dirty. I took a shower for an hour, but I still felt dirty. What I had promised myself would not happen until I was married had just happened.

My life was a merry-go-round. I continued to drink and drive, thinking I was a better driver when I had been drinking. I blamed the professors for my bad grades. I blamed my parents and friends for the fights. I thought they were always against me. I managed to go to church, but hung over. All along, I continued to deny that alcohol had any effect on my life.

Then it happened! I found out that God has a great sense of humor. He presented me with a senior internship at an alcoholism agency working in the problem drinkers' clinic. Once I started learning about the devastating effects of alcohol, my eyes were slowly opened. I was like a sponge soaking up everything except alcohol. My friends at school were wondering why I wasn't partying anymore. I used the excuse that my job kept me out too late and up too early.

I took a very close look at myself and three things struck me the most:
1) Experiencing blackouts - not remembering what I did although behaving "normally."
2) Having an increase in tolerance - drinking more than I used to.

3) Questioning whether my drinking was "normal."
I decided that I was just a "social drinker" and didn't drink any more or less than my friends.

When I had college behind me, I returned home. Unfortunately I started partying again, but it was not the same. My education had spoiled drinking for me. People became uncomfortable around me because I was always talking about what I had learned about alcohol.

God continued to work in His amazingly strange but wonderful way. My first full-time job was at the alcoholism agency where I had interned. Part of my job training was to attend AA and Al-anon meetings. Wow, what an experience! I already had a "higher power," God, but still I didn't have a relationship with Jesus. The people in those rooms, however, were examples of kind and loving people who were trying to get their lives together. Some of them admitted that they were powerless over alcohol and that their lives had become unmanageable. That was me! I was seeing people's lives changed because they were willing to take a look at their drinking and let Jesus Christ help them. I did too! Miracles were all around.

It has now been 21 years since I stopped drinking. Praise God! Am I an alcoholic? I don't know, but I'm not willing to start drinking to find out. I met my husband through my work, and we have three healthy children. We still have problems like everyone else, but my brain is no longer drugged by alcohol! Life is good!

I accepted a relationship with Jesus 10 years ago and life has "never been the same." I have joy that is over-flowing because I know that Jesus loves me and He has forgiven me for my past. What an awesome God we have never to give up on us! I make it my job to stay close to Him by staying in the Bible, meeting with Christian friends, worshiping and praying, praying, praying. It's a great joy to awaken each day and know that I am in the comfort of my loving Lord and Savior, Jesus Christ!

I would encourage anyone who is on a merry-go-round, or who is watching someone who is, to seek help. Alcohol abuse and alcoholism never get any better. It only gets worse until the person seeks help. Don't be afraid to ask. Enabling, bailing people out, and not allowing them to suffer the true consequences are not helping them with the problem. Find Christ centered programs. His grace will make a difference!

Jesus will never give up on you...
make Him your first choice!
*Joy Burst Beautiful Bonnie, Ohio*

*I said to the Lord,*
*You are my Lord;*
*apart from you*
*I have no good thing.*
*Psalm 16:2*

# Throw a Plastic Surgery Party

## Joy Buster

**Be Joyful!**
**Who me? How am I going to explain this**
**charge card bill? How did it get so high,**
**again?**

## Joy Booster

"Why wait? Buy now; Pay later" encourages people to
maneuver their finances around until they get *things*
that make them happy. Unfortunately, it doesn't take
long to find something even more satisfying, and the
bills keep coming. Plastic imprisonment can cause
devastation in families. Being tempted to overspend is
not a sin, but the acting on that temptation is. Trying to
find contentment in possessions can interrupt fellowship with your eternal treasure, Jesus Christ. For,
whatever occupies your thoughts
and time, that is where your
real treasure is.

Break out of debt bondage. Lock up the joy-killers of overspending. Ask God to help you gain His perspective on your situation. ***Grab Joy and Go!***

## Joy Injection

*But store up for yourselves treasures in heaven,*
*where moth and rust do not destroy,*
*and where thieves do not break in and steal.*
*For where your treasure is,*
*there your heart will be also.*
*Matthew 6:20-21*

## Joy Connection

Father, I need Your help,
I praise You for the real joy I find in...
Forgive me for...
Help me to make a difference today by...

# You came into this world with nothing. What are you taking with you when you die?

# To Dust or Not To Dust

## Joy Buster

**Be Joyful!**
**Who me? It's stressful maintaining the "house-beautiful" look!**

## Joy Booster

Do people come to visit you to see your dustless, perfectly decorated house? Or do people just stop in because they can experience a warm and caring attitude, a place of security and trust, and the comfort in your outstretched arms? Do they enjoy a relaxed atmosphere where they can talk and have fun? Let your home reflect your personality. Make your "welcome mat" mean what it says. Satan is pleased when your priorities of "I don't have time to do that, I've got to clean" deprives you of fellowship with others and with your Lord. When Christ is in your home and your heart, joy is always there, even if the windows are dirty! ***Grab joy and Go.***

## Joy Injection

*But the worries of life…*
*and the desires for other things take over.*
*They choke the word so that it can't produce anything.*
*Mark 4:19 GW*

## Joy Connection

Heavenly Friend and Head of my Family,
I praise You for the real joy I find in…
Forgive me for…
Help me to make a difference today by…

**Is your house
five-star quality?
Is it sturdy with faith,
clean with purity,
airy with hope,
insured with trust
and entertained
with joy?**
Fun Nun

# To Stress or De-stress

## ▬ Joy Buster

**Be Joyful!**
**Who me? Everything makes me feel**
**stressed, everything!**

## ▬ Joy Booster

When you are in the middle of a stressful situation,
don't always judge the circumstances by what you see.
The very thing that could look like your worst problem
may be what Jesus uses to deliver you. The disciples
were stressed and afraid. Their boat was in a storm,
but worse, they thought they saw a ghost. In reality, it
was not an added problem. It was actually their
salvation; Jesus was walking on the water. He did
this to demonstrate His power and His
protection. He showed them
there was no trial that He
could not penetrate!
If you are trying to
handle a stressful
situation by yourself,
give it up!

203

Faith looks up, but fear looks around! De-stress in Him! He is your hope, peace, and joy in even the slightest stress. ***Grab Joy and Go de-stress.***

## Joy Injection

*For my thoughts are not your thoughts,*
*neither are your ways my ways, declares the Lord.*
*Isaiah 55:8*

## Joy Connection

Jesus, Calmer of my stress,
I praise You for the real joy I find in...
Forgive me for...
Help me to make a difference today by...

**Stressed spelled backward
is desserts.
Life is uncertain.
Eat desserts first!**

# JOY Burst

## Be Joyful?
### Yes I can, even when...

Ever since I was a kid, I have loved music. I make a joyful noise wherever I go. I whistle, hum, sing, snap, click, tap or shuffle, letting the JOY of the Lord flow in and out of my heart.

Being legally blind has given me a real appreciation for the beauty of sound. That's probably what has kept me going all these years. Whenever I feel down, sad, lonely or depressed, I start a tune in my mind; it may be a slow, sad tune at first but soon the tempo picks up. Before I know it, the sound comes out of my mouth praising God with that joyful noise. Music can't change the circumstances of life, but it surely can make life a lot more enjoyable.

I was born with Optic Nerve Atrophy. I have 20/400 in my right eye and no reading capability in my left eye. I used to ask God, "Why did You make me give up so much?" But as I grew in my faith and trust in God, I learned that He has the perfect plan for my life even with this challenge. I accepted that my eyes were not going to change. I changed my attitude and my focus. My pity party became an exciting mission field! I rejoice every time He gives me an opportunity to reach out and encourage others or just whistle a happy tune! Try it!

There is always reason to rejoice!
*Joy Burst Linda Bailey, Alabama*

*Hope*

*Be joyful in hope;
patient in affliction,
faithful in prayer.
Romans 12:12*

# Trials

## ▰▰▰ Joy Buster

**Be Joyful!**
**Who me? I don't think I can. I've come to the end of my rope! I can't take any more. Why me?**

## ▰▰▰ Joy Booster

Job, a man of great faith, asked that question too. He didn't always see God's presence in his suffering even though he did recognize that God was in control. Eventually, Job was blessed with twice as much as he had. He saw the 4th generation of his children and died "fully aged." Discover, as Job did, a *new place of intimacy* with God that you could never know without suffering. Your past faith walk can nurture hope for the future. *Grab Joy and Go!*

## Joy Injection

*We were not completely wiped out.*
*His compassion is never limited.*
*It is new every morning. His faithfulness is great.*
*Lamentations 3:22-23 GW*

## Joy Connection

Dear Comforter,
I praise You for the real joy I find in...
Forgive me for...
Help me to make a difference today by...

**One Christian who has been tried**
**is worth a hundred who have not,**
**for the blessing of God**
**grows in trials.**
**He who has experienced them**
**can teach, and advise many**
**in bodily and spiritual matters.**

Martin Luther

# Unconditional Love? What's the Catch?

## Joy Buster

**Be Joyful!**
**Who me? I'm having a bad day. I've been**
**grouchy with the neighbors, my friends,**
**people in traffic, sales people at the store,**
**and even my innocent children. I don't love**
**myself today and I don't think anyone else**
**does either!**

## Joy Booster

People say that when they are having a good day in
life, they can really feel God's love. It's almost
tangible. But, on a bad day it is a very different story.
Not only do they not love
themselves, they find it impossible
that God would either.
We have so little
experience with
*unconditional*
*love—*

something we do not deserve—that we find it baffling. Rejoice! God's grace is not dependent on our performance nor is it rationed out in proportion to our goodness and badness on any given day. God's capacity is linked to the fact that He is love. Love is God's occupation and preoccupation, His mission and His favorite pastime! You cannot lose God's love by what you do or don't do. He overflows with *amazing grace* and loves you no matter what! This should ignite an attitude of gratitude! ***Grab Joy and Go share His grace!***

## Joy Injection

*For it is by grace you have been saved,*
*through faith—and this not from yourselves,*
*it is the gift of God—not by works,*
*so that no one can boast.*
*Ephesians 2:8-9*

## Joy Connection

God of Grace and God of Glory,
I praise You for the real joy I find in...
Forgive me for...
Help me to make a difference today by...

## Grace arranges tomorrow and sustains you today.

# Unlimited Supplies Await You!

## Joy Buster

**Be Joyful!**
**Who me? I've searched everywhere, and no store has what I want.**

## Joy Booster

One day a mother and daughter were shopping in a fabric store. The daughter found something she knew the mother must have. It was a bolt of ribbon with the word "joy" printed everywhere. The mother was ecstatic. She almost became a joy burst at that moment. The sales attendant asked, "How much joy do you want?" The mother wanted to purchase the entire reel but didn't want to seem greedy. After all, someone else might be looking for joy too. She settled for 5 yards. "What are you going to do with all this joy?" asked the clerk. "I don't know but I have been looking

211

everywhere for joy," replied Mother. "Now that I have found it, I think I'll save it. I might not find anymore joy!" Unlike manufactured joy, God's authentic joy is always available. No need to hoard or skimp. You can use it and share it and give it away – and there's *always more! So Grab God's Joy and Go empowered.*

## Joy Injection

*If I make you light-bearers, you don't think*
*I'm going to hide you under a bucket, do you?*
*I'm putting you on a light stand.*
*Now that I've put you there on a hilltop,*
*on a light stand—shine! Keep open house;*
*be generous with your lives. By opening up to others,*
*you'll prompt people to open up with God,*
*this generous Father in heaven.*
*Matthew 5:15-16 MSG*

## Joy Connection

Heavenly Enabler,
I praise You for the real joy I find in...
Forgive me for...
Help me to make a difference today by...

## One who is filled with joy preaches without preaching.

Mother Teresa

# Waiting and Weathering

### Joy Buster

**Be Joyful!**
**Who me? I don't like waiting because I've**
**got other things to do!**

### Joy Booster

In England the clay diggers leave the newly dug clay exposed to the weather for at least a year to make it more pliable. Much like the clay, we often need to be weathered for a while before we are ready for use. Moses was exposed to the weather during his life in Midian before God could use him. Jacob spent 20 years under Laban's abuse before he was sufficiently weathered. Joseph, too, was weathered from the time he was 17 until he was 30. In reality, waiting is part of life! What you may perceive as a delay in answers to your "I want it now" prayers is actually God's powerful and perfect timing.

213

You may have to search to find happiness, but joy is available in your weathering process. *His blessings never stop!* Joyfully anticipate them while you weather!! ***Grab Joy and Go!***

## Joy Injection

*The eyes of all look to you,*
*and you give them their food at the proper time.*
*Psalm 145:15*

## Joy Connection

Good Shepherd,
I praise You for the real joy I find in...
Forgive me for...
Help me to make a difference today by...

**Do something while you wait –
read God's Word. It will give strength
to rise above the pressures of life that would
otherwise squelch your joy.**

# JOY Burst

## Be Joyful?
### Yes I can, even when...

My Christian faith gives me constant reason to be joyous! Years ago I had emergency surgery with no time to make preparations. Diagnosis: Acute Pancreatitis. Prognosis: usually fatal. The surgeon told my husband that they had lost my pulse while I was on the operating table, but they revived me. He had done all he could, and I was now in God's hands.

I was heavily sedated in ICU for a week. Each time I awakened I saw my husband and my pastor praying over me. After a week I was transferred to the isolation unit and the nurses cheered. I was the only patient in ICU that week that had survived. Fighting infection and pain, I was finally discharged three weeks later to go home and face a 12-month recovery.

Thoughts kept racing through my mind...I'm a Christian Day School teacher. My husband and I have family devotions. I'm very close to God. Why is this happening to me?

I asked God to let me see our three children grow up – at least graduate from college. Then, all of a sudden it hit me – I can't make deals with God. He has a plan for my life. He is in control! With faith and hope I learned to rejoice in all things - even pain, suffering, challenges and hardships.

When I awake each morning, I thank God for the gift of another day, for being with me in the past and in each tomorrow. Each breath He gives me provides another opportunity to joyfully serve others and bring glory to Him. I have reason to be joyful and you do too!

Experience contentment in God's presence!
*Joy Burst Connie Kruelle, Maryland*

*Because of the Lord's great love*
*we are not consumed,*
*for His compassions never fail.*
*They are new every morning;*
*great is your faithfulness.*
*The Lord is good to those whose hope*
*is in him, to the one who seeks him.*
*Lamentations 3:22-23,25*

# Whine, Whine, Whine

## ▰▰ Joy Buster

**Be Joyful!**
**Who me, how can I when my clothes are**
**getting a little too snug, I have piles of**
**laundry, aching muscles, a huge heating bill,**
**just to name a few of my joy-robbers? I**
**know – whine, whine, whine!**

## ▰▰ Joy Booster

Isn't it amazing how thankfulness fluctuates with circumstances or feelings? To give thanks in all things often goes against your natural inclinations. Stop and raise your praise. Snug clothing could be from having plenty to eat. Laundry accumulates from having loved ones nearby. Aches and pains could mean you've been productive. Heating bills must mean you aren't living outside in the cold. Make a conscious decision to look at life through Christ-like eyes and joy-framed glasses. *Grab Joy and Go!*

217

## Joy Injection

*Thank God no matter what happens.*
*This is the way God wants you*
*who belong to Christ Jesus to live.*
*1 Thessalonians 5:18 MSG*

## Joy Connection

Dearest Jesus giver of ceaseless love,
I praise You for the real joy I find in...
Forgive me for...
Help me to make a difference today by...

**It is not always easy
being a joyful woman.
Most of us are more experienced
in grumbling than glowing.
Taper off your whining
so you don't get attitude whiplash.**

Barbara Johnson

# Who Me, A Joy-Filled Cracked Pot?

### ▰▰▰ Joy Buster

**Be Joyful!**
**Who me? How could I be a difference maker?**

### ▰▰▰ Joy Booster

A water bearer had two large pots, which hung on the pole he carried across his neck. One pot was perfect. The other was cracked. The cracked pot was ashamed of its own imperfections and miserable that it was only able to accomplish half of what it had been made to do. "I'm a bitter failure. I always lose half of my load. Because of my flaws you have to do all of this work and you don't get full value from your efforts." said the pot. The water bearer felt sorry for the cracked pot. "As we return to the master's house I want you to notice there are beautiful flowers only along one side of the path. That is because I have always known about your flaw and I took advantage of it. I planted flower seeds on your side of the path, and every day while we walked back from the stream, you have watered them. Because of your flaw I've been able to pick flowers to decorate my master's table. Without you, just the way you are, he would not have this beauty to grace his house."*

You can make a difference along life's journey. There is nothing insignificant that you do in Christ's name that goes unnoticed by the Lord. You make an impact! Electrifying! Avoid Satan's discouragement. Fill up daily with God's joyful Word. Vessels cannot pour anything out if they first haven't been filled. You are on a mission for the Lord. Be ecstatic! ***Grab Joy and Go make a difference.***

\*Story Source Unknown

## Joy Injection

*If you only look at us, you might well miss the*
*brightness. We carry this precious Message around*
*in the unadorned clay pots of our ordinary lives.*
*That's to prevent anyone from confusing*
*God's incomparable power with us.*
*2 Corinthians 4:7 MSG*

## Joy Connection

Enabling Heavenly Father,
I praise You for the real joy I find in...
Forgive me for...
Help me to make a difference today by...

**The joy of walking in God's plan,**
**is to know you can bloom**
**wherever you are planted.**

## Be Joyful?
### Yes I can, even when...

I know about stress. I'm a mother! I could hardly eat, sleep or think clearly because I had heard that my newborn son was to be killed. I was distraught so I hid him and trusted in God.

God overwhelmed me with blessings. Moses was safe in his basket boat; Pharaoh's daughter found him and she even let me nurse her newfound infant.* God's purpose in all these events (which I thought were tragedies at the time) would later help Moses become a great leader.

I know that motherhood is challenging! I encourage you to marinate in God's Word daily, saturate yourself with His grace and never stop praying for your children. Let Jesus handle the things in life that are beyond your control, even the people and hurts that tend to obliterate your joy. Be assured that He can keep up with your pace and your prayers!

Only through Him did I find contentment in desperation. You can too! When I reflect on God's grace I always become a joy burst. Does this happen to you too?

*Exodus 2

Be a Joy-Spreader about God's grace!
*Joy Burst Jochebed, Heaven*

*God is our refuge and strength, and ever-present help in trouble. Psalm 46:1*

# Who's In Charge?

## ▰▰▰ Joy Buster

**Be Joyful!**
**Who me? I'm exhausted from fighting the personal storms in my life.**

## ▰▰▰ Joy Booster

One day a little girl was on an airplane flight when the plane got caught in some very bad turbulence. The plane pitched back and forth and dipped up and down. Trays were sliding everywhere. People were scared and screaming. In the middle of all this chaos, the little girl kept on playing and even giggling "Whee!" as if nothing was wrong. The woman sitting next to her asked, "How can you play and be happy at a time like this?" She replied, "Oh, it's easy, my daddy is the pilot."*

If we want our lives to flow with joy, then we have to *look* for the Lord's fingerprints in the midst of whatever is happening.

However dismal or intimidating our circumstances may seem, we can find some indication that He is with us. Only then will we be able to "leap for joy," as Jesus urged, because we'll be looking past the hardship to focus on our great reward: the Lord Himself. Every impossible storm is accompanied by unique opportunities for joy from His presence. *Grab Joy and Go!*

*Story source Unknown

### Joy Injection

> *Immediately he [Jesus] spoke to them and said,*
> *"Take courage! It is I. Don't be afraid."*
> *Then he climbed into the boat with them,*
> *and the wind died down.*
> *They were completely amazed.*
> *Mark 6:50b-51a*

### Joy Connection

Father, my forever Pilot,
I praise You for the real joy I find in...
Forgive me for...
Help me to make a difference today by...

## Do you risk enough to exercise your faith?

# Wipe My Tears

## Joy Buster

**Be Joyful!**
**Who me? I'm devastated. My tears are**
**endless. I have no joy!**

## Joy Booster

It seems that sorrow strikes at the most inopportune
time, yet is there ever a right time? Bitter despair may
press down so hard that you seem to lose your ability
to keep life in perspective. Let your tears flow. Jesus
wept too! God will provide the grace that will carry
you through the hard times and turn disappointments
into glorious victories. Trust that God is not only *near*
you, He is *with* you! Let
His Spirit renew your
mind to see your
circumstances as God
sees them. Live
in the joy of His
presence.

225

Receive His *genuine* peace and the comfort that only He can give. ***Grab Joy and Go in grace!***

## Joy Injection

*Long enough I've carried this ton of trouble,*
*lived with a stomach full of pain.*
*I've thrown myself headlong into your arms—*
*I'm celebrating your rescue.*
*Psalm 13:2a, 5 MSG*

## Joy Connection

Heavenly Father, giver of inner peace,
I praise You for the real joy I find in...
Forgive me for...
Help me to make a difference today by...

# "Why do human beings rush around and worry? You would think they had no Heavenly Father," said the robin to the sparrow.

## Be Joyful?
### Yes I can, even when...

After my husband died, I was plagued with the "if onlys." If only I had insisted on calling the doctor when he started feeling sick. If only I had recognized the symptoms of an oncoming heart attack. If only I had told him how much I loved him when he left for work that fateful morning. If only we had spent more time together, just the two of us. If only – I hadn't said...If only...If only... - day after day.

I seemed to remember every minor disagreement we had ever had. In my mind, they were all my fault. My husband was on a pedestal and perfect. Then one day, as I was driving home from work, I began sharing an "if only" with the Lord. Suddenly it dawned on me, "But he said...." It was the Lord bringing me back to reality. In that instant, I realized once again that my husband was human, too.

With that reawakened understanding, I could at last move from grief to a life filled once more with joy in Christ. Because my husband was a believer, I knew he

*Hope*

was enjoying eternity with the Lord. Now I could fully accept the fact that I am a forgiven child of God.

God keeps His promises to be with us!
*Joy Burst Marlys Taege Moberg,
Wisconsin*

*May the God of hope fill you with all joy and peace
as you trust in him,
so that you may overflow with hope
by the power of the Holy Spirit.
Romans 15:13*

# Worry? I've Got To!

███ Joy Buster

**Be Joyful!**
**Who me? How can I when I have so many**
**things to worry about?**

███ Joy Booster

When you've worried about things before, has it ever improved or changed the situation? Satan delights in having you think you can control circumstances by spending your time thinking about how you can "fix" the problem. Get away Satan! Turn your worries over to the *only* One who wants to take away your every care. It's God's grace that desires to do this for you! But remember, once you release your concerns, *do not* grab them back, not even when God's not on your time table! Let joy fashion your day! ***Grab Joy and go!***

███ Joy Injection

*Cast your cares on the Lord and he will sustain you;*
*he will never let the righteous fall.*
*Psalm 55:22*

## ▇▇▇ Joy Connection

Dear Jesus, carrier of my burdens,
I praise You for the real joy I find in...
Forgive me for...
Help me to make a difference today by...

## God works from the inside out; the devil works from the outside in.

## JOY-Toon

Thank you
Doctor!
I have
Joy-itis!!!!

# JOY Burst

## Be Joyful?
### Yes I can, even when...

"How can this happen in my family? I feel so help-less!" These thoughts swirled through my mind as my son and daughter-in-law started having problems in their marriage. Like any mother, I prayed that my grandsons would have a strong family foundation. Unfortunately, I had to accept the fact that separation was a reality.

God then spoke to me through a Christian friend whose daughter had divorced several years before. My friend was experiencing the same feelings and asking God the same kind of questions that I did, but now she could see things differently. She encouraged me to do this too.

My friend explained that now her grandchildren were closer to her both geographically and emotional-ly. She could also help out whenever the children had an appointment, take part in their school events and provide stability while their mother worked. She was thrilled to put God's love in action on a daily basis. I praise God for my friend who helped me see sunshine through the storm clouds.

I was assured once again that God was in control, and good does come from even devastating circumstances. I was convinced of this after my life-threatening auto accident. People brought food, helped out in numerous ways, prayed for my recovery and offered those most needed words of encouragement. Once again God was using people to give me a new perspective! Who is He using in your life?

God's promises are always assuring!
*Joy Burst God's Child, North Carolina*

*Guide me in your truth and teach me,*
*for you are God my Savior,*
*and my hope is in you all day long.*
*Psalm 25:5*

# Worthless or Not?

## ▰▰▰ Joy Buster

**Be Joyful!**
**Who Me? I'm tired of measuring up to**
**society standards. Why can't I have worth**
**by just being me?**

## ▰▰▰ Joy Booster

Crumple a dollar bill. Squeeze it. Put it on the ground
and stomp on it. Roll it in dirt and cover it with mud!
Does that bill still have the same value even after all
that? Yes. Even though its condition changed, the
value was not lost. When you experience trials, testing
and tragedies, you have not lost your value as God's
child. Your worth is not in what
you do, or who you know, but
in whose you are! Happiness
is not permanent, but the joy of
the Lord is always there in a
believer's life! You are
*never without the presence*
of your Savior. Nothing
can take away the real

233

joy He offers or the value He sees in you. Celebrate –
through Christ, you are a woman of worth! *Grab Joy
and Go!*

## Joy Injection

*I'm absolutely convinced that nothing —
nothing living or dead, angelic or demonic,
today or tomorrow, high or low,
thinkable or unthinkable — absolutely nothing
can get between us and God's love
because of the way that Jesus
our Master has embraced us.
Romans 8:38-39 MSG*

## Joy Connection

Holy One of God,
I praise You for the real joy I find in...
Forgive me for...
Help me to make a difference today by...

## You are God's idea.
## That's a joy burst thought.

Annetta E. Dellinger

# JOY Burst

## Be Joyful?
### Yes I can, even when...

Once, while sharing photos of my best friend and me, a child in my Sunday school class commented, "Gee, Mrs. Hurta, you look like you were a real brain!" I was amused and embarrassed. I wondered what gave it away? Was it the glasses and sensible shoes? The plain—not cute—face? Does intelligence have a look? I'm not sure, but I feel like a real lone star sometimes. All I ever wanted was to please God and be like every-one else – likeable, helpful, productive, part of the group but not intimidating. Brainy kids have feelings too!

As a kid I never had to study hard. I knew all the answers but I thought the kids were thinking that I was a know-it-all—a teacher's pet. I often held back, partly to allow the other students the satisfaction of partici-pating in the class, but mostly because I didn't like being different. People seemed to shy away from me. I began to hesitate to share my knowledge and talent. When offered friendship I was afraid that I might not live up to their expectations.

I am far from perfect; Nearly failing advanced math in high school helped to refocus my interest in developing my artistic talents. That was a painful experience but I am confident that God was guiding me! Each failure in my life serves to broaden my understanding of myself and increase my appreciation for others' strengths and gifts, so that I rely more on

God's wisdom: *Search me, O God, and know my heart; test me and know my anxious thoughts.* (Psalm 139:23)

As I have gotten older and studied God's Word, I realize that we each have the exact DNA makeup that God prescribed for us and a purpose to fulfill. He had planned a way for me to glorify Him through the gifts He gave me creativity, compassion, leadership and organization.

Time and experience have taught me to be bold about sharing my creative gifts. God has opened doors to use my talents to share his mission for our church. My graphic artwork and watercolor paintings now bring inspiration and funding for mission endeavors.

Give your uniqueness a chance to sparkle for Jesus. He designed you for a special purpose in His Kingdom that no one else can fulfill. Gifts, great or small, give glory to our God. Be a bright star for Jesus!

You are God's Idea!
*Joy Burst Janet Hurta, Texas*

*I praise you for I am fearfully and wonderfully made; your works are wonderful, I know that full well.*
*Psalm 139:14*

# Write, Right Now

### ■■■■ Joy Buster

**Be Joyful!**
**Who me? Right now I could use some**
**encouragement.**

### ■■■■ Joy Booster

Open your Bible and read God's encouraging words.
His encouragement is like a pebble thrown into water.
While there is always an immediate impact, the ripples
continue indefinitely. When you have been encouraged, pass on the energized feeling. *Encouragement is
infectious.* Yield to the nudges of the Spirit when
someone's name comes into your mind. Don't put it

off. Write that note. Make that
call. Say that kind word.
Provide a listening ear.
Say a prayer and
give a hug.

Smiles can cover up many pains. Give affirmation as if there were no tomorrow. Be jubilant about how God will use you to uplift others. ***Grab Joy and Go!***

## Joy Injection

*He comes alongside us*
*when we go through hard times,*
*and before you know it,*
*he brings us alongside someone else*
*who is going through hard times*
*so that we can be there for that person*
*just as God was there for us.*
*2 Corinthians 1:4 MSG*

## Joy Connection

O Creator of encouragement,
I praise You for the real joy I find in...
Forgive me for...
Help me to make a difference today by...

**Compassion is difficult to give away
because it keeps coming back.**

# Yes, I Love Videos!

## Joy Buster

**Be Joyful!**
**Who Me? Say no to a free video, I don't**
**think so...well, that depends on what's on it.**

## Joy Booster

A van has just pulled up in front of your home. The driver knocks on your door and says, "This is a free video just for you!" With curiosity you read the title, "This Is Your Life" and play it immediately. It contains every detail about you...your first breath, first tooth, first step, all the people you have ever known, each word you have ever said (good and bad), every secret thought you had and would not want anyone to know, places you've been, things you've done, clothes you've worn, books read, music played, TV watched.... It even shows each strand of hair ever left in your comb. There is not one thing missing from this video about you!

How many people would you show the video of your life to? Probably no one. Yet, *Jesus already knows every detail about your life and He still loves you!* Ponder that thought. WOW, what an awesome,

forgiving, loving God
you have. He loved you
before you were born. He loved you when you proved
yourself to be sinfully disobedient to Him. He even
loved you this week when you disappointed Him. His
love is ongoing. He doesn't just say *I love you*, like
others do - He proved it when His Son died on the
cross for your sins and rose again. Do you know
anyone else who loves you so much that they would
die for you? Understand it or not, you can enjoy God's
love. Live in the light of that. Trust God's love
and Jesus' sacrifice. Allow Him to restore your

significance to you through faith in Christ Jesus.
These are dynamite joy-filled thoughts, aren't they?
***Grab Joy and Go praise God from whom all
blessings flow!***

## Joy Injection

*I have loved you with an everlasting love....*
*Jeremiah 31:3*

*Jesus said, If you hold to my teaching,
you are really my disciples.
Then you will know the truth,
and the truth will set you free.*
*John 8:31-32*

## Joy Connection

Jesus Christ, the only One who constantly
loves me,
I praise You for the real joy I find in...
Forgive me for...
Help me to make a difference today by...

**We have hope beyond this life because of the
Savior who walked out of His grave!
For that reason alone, we ought to be,
of all people, most celebrative!**

Dale Craw Shaw

# Yes! Now I Understand!

## Joy Buster

**Be Joyful!**
**Who Me? Yes I can always be joyful, even if**
**I'm not happy!**

Now I understand the meaning of real joy. *Joy is in the presence of God in my life and in my personal relationship with Jesus Christ!* Satan, take your bag of doubts, discouragement, anxiety, worry, fear, anger, bitterness, hopelessness, negative attitudes, and everything else you use to rob my focus from the perfect love of my Lord and Savior, Jesus Christ. **There is always hope in the good times and the bad!** Satan, you joy buster, hear this: There is no doubt in my mind that **I CAN find real joy in this joy-starved world because I am ALWAYS in Jesus everlasting presence…in His EVERLASTING love…and Jesus will NEVER leave me, ever!**

242

I have inner peace, contentment, and confidence that **I can tackle the joy busters in my life because my joy booster is looking forward to eternal life in heaven!**

## Joy Booster

Have FAITH in the Lord. TRUST in your Savior, Jesus Christ. BELIEVE through the power of the Holy Spirit. BE IN God's Word daily and then you can always ***Be Joyful! Who Me? Yes you!***

## Joy Injection

*Jesus said to His disciples [you],*
*"I have told you this so that MY JOY may be IN YOU*
*and that YOUR JOY may be complete!"*
*John 15:11*

*You make the path of life known to me.*
*COMPLETE joy is in YOUR PRESENCE.*
*Pleasures are by your side forever!*
*Psalm 16:11 GW*

## Joy Connection

Father, Son, and Holy Spirit, may Your inspired words written in this book's Joy-Spirations be used to bring a new perspective to the reader and glorify You. Open the hearts of the readers to find the reality of spiritual joy which only You offer. Thank You for enabling those who have shared their personal stories to become Joy Bursts of Hope for us! Empower us through your Holy Spirit to Grab Joy and Go. Be contagious with God's JOY! *Amen*

*Annetta E Dellinger*
Author and Joy Burst for the Lord!

*Be a vessel for the Lord.*
*Pour out His Love to others,*
*In your own unique way.*

# Grab Joy and Go!

# Books by Annetta Dellinger

Be Joyful! Who Me? Daily Joy-Spirations for Women
Celebrate! You Are A Woman of Worth
Mug Meditations
Lead Me Lord Through...Motherhood
Ann Elizabeth Signs With Love
The Jesus Tree
Children's Bulletin Idea Book
Creative Science for Young Children
Adopted and Loved Forever
Chuckles and Challenges
Creative Games for Young Children
Angels Are My Friends
Happy Birthday Jesus
Colors, Colors Everywhere
Hugging
My First Easter
More Happy Talk
Special Holiday Handbook
Easter Handbook
Good Manners for God's Children
I Talk to God
You Are Special to Jesus
Bible Code Book Series of 4
God's Little Children Series of 4
Cause God Made Me That Way
Happy Talk